Daniel

THE MARTIN BUBER LIBRARY

The Martin Buber Library

Daniel: Dialogues on Realization
Maurice Friedman, trans.; Paul Mendes-Flohr, intro.

Ecstatic Confessions: The Heart of Mysticism
Esther Cameron, trans.; Paul Mendes-Flohr, ed.

The First Buber: Youthful Zionist Writings of Martin Buber
Gilya G. Schmidt, trans. and ed.

Gog and Magog: A Novel
Ludwig Lewisohn, trans.

Israel and the World: Essays in a Time of Crisis

The Letters of Martin Buber: A Life of Dialogue
Richard and Clara Winston and Harry Zohn, trans;
Nahum N. Glatzer and Paul Mendes-Flohr, eds.

Martin Buber: A Contemporary Perspective
Paul Mendes-Flohr, ed.

Martin Buber and Feminist Ethics: The Priority of the Personal
James W. Walters

Martin Buber on Psychology and Psychotherapy:
Essays, Letters, and Dialogue
Judith Buber Agassi, ed.; Paul Roazen, intro.

On the Bible: Eighteen Studies
Nahum N. Glatzer, ed.; Harold Bloom, intro.

On Zion: The History of an Idea
Stanley Godman, trans.; Nahum N. Glatzer, foreword

Paths in Utopia

Two Types of Faith
Norman P. Goldhawk, trans.; David Flusser, afterword

Daniel

DIALOGUES
ON REALIZATION

MARTIN BUBER

Translated from the German by
Maurice Friedman

With a New Introduction by
Paul Mendes-Flohr

SYRACUSE UNIVERSITY PRESS

First Syracuse University Press Edition 2018

18 19 20 21 22 23   6 5 4 3 2 1

First English translation copyright © 1964 by Holt, Rinehart and Winston, Inc.
Published in German under the title *Daniel, Die Gespräche von der
Verwirklichung*, by Insel-Verlag, Leipzig.
Author's Preface from Martin Buber, *Werke*, Vol. I, *Sclirßen zur Philosophie*.
Kösel-Verlag, Munich; Verlag Lambert Schneider, Heidelberg, 1962, page 1l.

∞ The paper used in this publication meets the minimum requirements of the
American National Standard for Information Sciences—Permanence of Paper for
Printed Library Materials, ANSI Z39.48-1992.

For a listing of books published and distributed by Syracuse University Press,
visit www.SyracuseUniversityPress.syr.edu.

ISBN: 978-0-8156-0947-6

Library of Congress Cataloging-in-Publication Data

Names: Buber, Martin, 1878–1965, author.
Title: Daniel : dialogues on realization / Martin Buber ; translated from
    the German by Maurice Friedman ; with a new introduction by Paul
    Mendes-Flohr.
Other titles: Daniel, Gespräche von der Verwirklichung. English
Description: First Syracuse University Press Edition. | Syracuse : Syracuse
    University Press, 2018. | Series: The Martin Buber library | Originally
    published: New York : Holt, Rinehart and Winston, 1964.
Identifiers: LCCN 2018035032 | ISBN 9780815609476 (pbk. : alk. paper)
Subjects: LCSH: Life. | Relationism. | Reality.
Classification: LCC B3213.B83 D33 2018 | DDC 181/.06—dc23 LC record
    available at https://lccn.loc.gov/2018035032

Printed in the United States of America

Contents

Author's Preface

After a descent during which I had to utilize without a halt the late light of a dying day, I stood on the edge of a meadow, now sure of the safe way, and let the twilight come down upon me. Not needing a support and yet willing to accord my lingering a fixed point, I pressed my stick against a trunk of an oak tree. Then I felt in twofold fashion my contact with being: here, where I held the stick, and there, where it touched the bark. Appearing to be only where I was, I nonetheless found myself there, too, where I found the tree.

At that time dialogue appeared to me. For the speech of man, wherever it is genuine speech, is like that stick; that means: truly directed address. Here, where I am, where ganglia and organs of speech help me to form and to send forth the word, here I "mean" him to whom I send it, I intend him, this one unexchangeable man. But also there, where he is, something of me is delegated, something that is not at all substantial in nature like that being-here, rather pure vibration and incomprehensible; that remains there, with him, the man meant by me, and takes part in the receiving of my word. I encompass him to whom I turn.

Introduction

Published in 1913 by perhaps Germany's most prestigious publishing house,[1] *Daniel* was celebrated in its day as a uniquely powerful philosophical poem. It is no longer read, undoubtedly because it was eclipsed a decade later by the publication of *I and Thou*,[2] which inaugurated Buber's philosophy of dialogue. To be sure, there are still occasional references to *Daniel*, even by some who have not read it. Although the distinctive religiosity advocated by Buber in *Daniel* and its "dialogues on realization" is not specifically Jewish, the title of the book has led some to believe otherwise. In the scroll accompanying an honorary doctorate Buber received in 1958 from the Sorbonne, he is lauded as the author of *Daniel*, a "great Jewish book" which gives pristine expression to Israel's prophetic "voice for justice . . . and redemption."[3] But Buber's *Daniel* has nothing to do with the biblical prophet.

The book's stylistic similarities to Nietzsche's *Zarathustra* suggest that Buber named his book and its principal protagonist Daniel after the biblical contemporary of the Persian seer Zarathustra. Indeed, as Gustav Landauer, Buber's close friend and in many respects his intellectual alter ego, noted, *Daniel* might at most be viewed as a response to Nietzsche's rhapsodic call for an Übermensch. Upon reviewing a draft of the first part of the volume, Landauer remarked in a letter to Buber that with *Daniel*, "you are achieving what Nietzsche did not achieve in his *Zarathustra*."[4] Focusing his comparison solely on matters of style and rhetoric, he notes the tension in Nietzsche's dialogue (characteristic of German didactic writing more generally) between the speaking subject's unreserved speech and "the speech of the soul," and credits Buber with overcoming this problematic narrative duality:

> I find this greatness in this portion of your book: the passion of the subject in the form of the language, which is shaped so that it is at once entirely the language of the speaker and entirely the speaking subject. In this work [that is, *Daniel*] about unity in duality you have achieved *what the work is all about*.[5]

Like many of his generation, Buber had clearly been inspired by Nietzsche's effort to create a new poetic language, a language grounded not so much in conceptually coherent argumentation, but instead representing the act of thinking itself in its "rhythmic diversity" and "corporeality of expression." Indeed, in *Daniel*, Buber allowed his thoughts to unfold dialectically and poetically, rather than analytically, and Landauer clearly viewed his eschewal of abstract discourse in favor of an evocative, poetic voice to be more successful than Nietzsche's own effort to do so.

Nonetheless, Landauer found that Buber occasionally allowed his poetic pathos to swirl out of control. Thus, he gently chided his friend: "The reader cannot immediately grasp everything you say; here and there you have little more than a grey, vague feeling, and in addition an attempt to make fixed terminology develop a life its own." As a result, Landauer continued, there are times that "I feel somewhat like a student who has unfortunately missed the early classes and who gathers from the definite tone that there are established terms which cannot be amended; but he has no experience with them or examples of them and is supposed to keep up and build on the basis of this."[6]

Buber would take Landauer's critique to heart. In his subsequent publications, he sought to heed Landauer's caveat and not allow his quest for a poetic idiom to obscure the philosophical message it was to evoke. He acknowledged the rhetorical infelicities and hence the occasional conceptual opaqueness of *Daniel*. His reluctance to have the volume reprinted, however, was largely due to the clarification of its "message" with the publication of *I and Thou* in 1923. In yielding to repeated requests by Maurice Friedman to translate *Daniel* into English, he explained: "*Daniel* is an early book in which there is already expressed the great duality of human life, but only in its cognitive and not yet in its communicative and existential character. This book is obviously a transition to a new type of thinking and must be characterised as such."[7]

Daniel is thus to be read as a work that anticipates, if but inchoately, the two fundamental modes of engaging reality which in his mature dialogical thought Buber calls the I-It and I-Thou attitudes. In *Daniel* this "great duality of life" is delineated as orientation and realization, respectively. In a letter to Max Brod, who understood *Daniel* as promoting a form of mysticism, Buber explained that this would be a misreading: "Realization is not ecstasy. Whereas ecstasy is episodic and isolating, realization is enduring and bonding. In realization knowledge and ethos meld. A person only knows the world through his deeds." Significantly, he refers Brod to a Daoist teaching of the Chinese sage Zhuang Zhou: "The knowledge the Consummate Person attains is not by virtue of his thoughts, but in his deeds."[8] By deeds Buber has in mind the Daoist concept of *woe-wie*—no-action, a nonintentional, non-calculating, non-deliberate manner of being in the world. In adhering to the "path" of *woe-wie* one is spontaneously and wholly open to the moment, the here and now.[9]

Buber would, however, eventually acknowledge that Brod's reading of *Daniel*'s "dialogues on realization" as pointing to a mystical sonship with God was not utterly a misreading. All Brod had to read was the volume's epigraph from the ninth-century Irish neoplatonic philosopher and poet Johannes Scotus Eriugena—*Deus in creatura mirabili et ineffabili modo creatur* (In a wondrous and ineffable way God is created)—God becomes, is realized, through his creatures.[10] Shortly after the publication of *I and Thou*, Buber wrote an essay in which he sought to clarify and correct "imprecise" formulations in his predialogical writings. With respect to "the concept of 'the realization of God' . . . [it] becomes inexact when . . . we say that God must be transmuted from an abstract truth into a reality; for this term lures us into a glittering notion that God is an idea which can become reality only through man, and, furthermore, induces the hopelessly wrong conception that God is not, but that He becomes—either within man or within mankind." Rather, "we should understand that to 'realize God' means to prepare the world for God as a place for His reality—to help the world to be God-real (*gottwirklich*)."[11] Indicatively, Buber would omit the Eriugena epigraph from all post-1923 editions of *Daniel* as well as emend some of the wording.[12]

Yet, as Grete Schaeder counsels, we would fail "to do justice" to *Daniel* "if we see it only as a preliminary stage of *I and Thou*."[13] In *Daniel*'s five dialogues (the German cast them as conversations [*Gespräche*]), Buber gives sustained expression to the Philosophy of Life (*Lebensphilosphie*)— its neo-Romantic vitalism, mystical pantheism and celebration of the creative, "authentic" personality—which had captured his imagination since his early days as a university student.[14] Accordingly, Schaeder identifies the overarching theme of Daniel's conversations as "centered around the concept of the quest for an uncompromising and heroic life."[15] Inspired by Nietzsche's injunction to "be one's self" (*sei du selbst*), Daniel affirms a life of radical intellectual and spiritual integrity, of the unbending resolve to be true to one's self. "This is the kingdom of God," Daniel explains to one of his interlocutors. It is "the kingdom of danger and risk, of eternal beginning and eternal becoming, of open spirit and deep realization, the kingdom of holy insecurity."[16] By leading a "heroic" life, unconditioned by social convention and the epistemological calculus by which one "orients" one's self "rationally" in the world, the hero serves to realize or to render God—who is not subject to the divisive spatial and temporal conditions of the world—manifest in our everyday life as the ultimate unifying, harmonizing force of reality. In the draft of the chapter (dialogue) in which this declaration was made, "On Meaning" (*Vom dem Sinn*), Buber contemplated giving it a subtitle, "On the Heroic Life" (*Vom herorische Leben*).[17]

Daniel's teaching is universal, addressed to each and every human being. We can strive to bring about the "fullness of time"—the Kingdom—only "in the course of fulfilling ourselves. Our trouble and what impels us on is not that time is unfilled but that we are unfulfilled."[18] Adhering to the path of *woe-wie*, "realization, thus, relates each event to nothing other than its own content and just thereby shapes it into a sign of the eternal (*Signum des Ewigen*)."[19] In "exalted solitude," the heroic individual "receives that which befalls him as a message (*Botschaft*); he does what is necessary as a task (*Auftrag*) and proclamation."[20] In realizing this task, "the life of the hero . . . is preserved as something precious and consecrated in itself . . . and elevated as a meaningful constellation in the heaven of inward existence (*Himmel des inneren Dasein*)."[21]

The heroic individual bears the existential risk attendant to defying the "security of the sleepwalker,"[22] the security wrought by an empirical and conventional orientation in the world. In realizing God in the deeds of non-action, the hero "realizes himself and all being."[23]

—Paul Mendes-Flohr

NOTES

For a comprehensive analysis of *Daniel*, one may consult: Maurice Friedman's introduction to his translation of *Daniel* (New York: Holt, Rinehart and Winston, 1964), 3–44; Shmuel Hugo Bergman, *Dialogical Philosophy from Kierkegaard to Buber*, trans. Arnold A. Gerstein (Albany: State University of New York Press, 1991), 217–26; Phil Huston, *Martin Buber's Journey to Presence* (New York: Fordham University Press, 2007), 106–84; Grete Schaeder, *The Hebrew Humanism of Martin Buber*, trans. Noah J. Jacobs (Detroit: Wayne University Press, 1973), 107–43; and Israel Koren, "Between Buber's *Daniel* and His *I and Thou*: A New Examination," *Modern Judaism* 22, no. 2 (May 2002): 169–98.

1. Martin Buber, *Daniel. Gespräche von der Verwirklichung* (Leipzig: Insel Verlag, 1913).

2. Martin Buber, *Ich und Du* (Leipzig: Insel Verlag, 1923).

3. The honorary degree, Docteur Honoris Causa, was awarded to Buber.

4. Landauer to Buber, July 25, 1925. *The Letters of Martin Buber*, eds. Nahum N. Glatzer and Paul Mendes-Flohr, trans. Richard Winston, Clara Winston, and Harry Zohn (New York: Schocken Books, 1991), 133.

5. Ibid., 134.

6. Landauer to Buber, September 9, 1912. *Letters*, 127–36.

7. The letter is cited in the translator's preface, *Daniel: Dialogues on Realization*, trans. Maurice Friedman (New York: Holt, Reinhart and Winston, 1964), n.p.

8. Buber to Max Brod, June 12, 1913. Buber, *Briefwechsel aus sieben Jahrzehnten* (Heidelberg: Verlag Lambert Schneider, 1972), vol. 1, 350f.

9. See Buber, "Die Lehre von Tao," Nachwort, *Reden und Gleichnisse der Tschuang-Tse*, ed. Martin Buber (Leipzig: Insel Verlag, 1910).

10. Johannis Scotti Eriugenae, *Periphyseon: (De divisione naturae)*, ed. I. P. Sheldon-Williams (Dublin: Dublin Institute for Advanced Studies, 1968–81), Book 3, Paragraph 17.

11. Martin Buber, Preface to the 1923 edition [*Reden über das Judentum*], *On Judaism*, ed. N. N. Glatzer (New York: Schocken Books, 1967), 8f.

12. These revisions are noted in the critical edition of *Daniel*. Cf. *Martin Buber Werkausgabe*, vol. 1: *Frühe Kulturkritische und Philosophie, 1891–1924*, ed. Martin Treml (Güterslohr: Gütersloher Verlagshaus, 2001), 183–235, 317–21.

13. Grete Schaeder, *The Hebrew Humanism of Martin Buber*, trans. Noah J. Jacobs (Detroit: Wayne State University Press, 1973), 119.

14. Reflecting on his early interest in pantheistic mysticism, Buber remarked, "Since 1900 I had first been under the influence of German mysticism from Meister Eckhart to Angelus Silesius, according to which the primal ground of being, the nameless impersonal Godhead, comes to 'birth' in the human soul." Buber, "Replies to My Critics," *The Philosophy of Martin Buber*, eds. Paul Arthur Schilpp and Maurice Friedman (LaSalle, Ill.: The Library of Living Philosophers, 1966), 689.

15. Grete Schaeder, "Martin Buber: A Biographical Sketch," in *The Letters of Martin Buber*, eds. Nahum N. Glatzer and Paul Mendes-Flohr, trans. Richard Winston, Clara Winston, and Harry Zohn (New York: Schocken Books, 1991), 25.

16. Buber, *Daniel*, 95.

17. Martin Buber, *Werkausgabe*, vol. 1, 204.

18. Buber to Hans Kohn, November 12, 1912. *The Letters of Martin Buber*, 140.

19. Buber, *Daniel*, 94; German text, 76.

20. Ibid., 95. I have emended the English translation.

21. Ibid., 94; German, 76.

22. Ibid.

23. Ibid. The Daoist doctrine of *woe-wie* would inform Buber's concept of the I-Thou encounter. Cf. "The You encounters me by grace—it cannot be found by seeking. But that I speak the basic word to it is a deed of my whole being, it is an essential deed. . . . Thus, the relationship is election and electing, passive and active at once. An action of the whole being must approach passivity, for it does away with all partial actions and thus with any sense of action . . ." Martin Buber, *I and Thou*, trans. Walter Kaufmann (New York: Charles Scribner's Sons, 1970), 57.

Daniel

I

On Direction

Dialogue in the Mountains

DANIEL: Let us go further. I take no pleasure in resting in the midst of the mountains. One must be able to remain upright, uphill, downhill, until one again stands in the valley and in the usual order. If we sit down up here, we shall have established the mastery of the plains in this place to which it should never reach. To me it is as if we injured the meaning of things. I am ashamed of my body which cannot preserve its steepness until it is achieved. The rocks tower in the air like a call, like an accusation. And only then do they become my brothers.

THE WOMAN: But in rising do you not feel all the more precipitously the revelation that it is granted you to climb? Are not the hollows of your knees made threefold happy to be permitted again to stretch? Again—that is the great jubilation of our lives. Would we not be miserable—creatures flung into a stale existence—if we were not born again every morning out of the abyss of sleep?

DANIEL: Yes, that is the breath of the earth, the indispensable. Because we cannot breathe like eternal beings who exhale the one, directionless world-breath, we make for ourselves out of the game of in and out a small sensual delight. Because we cannot circle above all existence—sleepless, unbroken, boundless, glowing—we content ourselves with being submerged and awakening. Because we cannot ascend into the spaceless . . .

THE WOMAN: Into the spaceless?

DANIEL: Into the spaceless! For it is that, indeed, that lifts and blesses us for climbing: that we liberate ourselves from the prison of direction-building. *Seem* to liberate ourselves, you may say. But I cannot measure my life-experience by a more valid reality when it has been for me the most valid of all. I still know how it happened to me the first time. What happened? A crossbeam detached itself from the cross of the space to which I was bound, and soon my feet were also free: I stood up free in the vertical, and I was the vertical. For only now did I feel in truth the meaning of my upright body, my upright body-soul. I lifted my arms above my head in order to intensify still further this uprightness, and soon the flames beat upward from my heels to my fingernails, and no cathedral's buttress ever stood with such extended life as I.

THE WOMAN: I sense it, Daniel, what you say, and as something slumbering, dreaming in me. But how can you think of this triumph of penetrating space as an ascent into the spaceless?

DANIEL: Is not space the clearest form of the great occurrence in which the One is intersected by the Many? And is not this, our way, a passionate image of that free enduring in the One that is denied us?

Certainly, what I experienced as I stood uplifted between heaven and earth was still space and had to remain such; but reflected therein was a kingdom in which there is nothing except my self and over it its completion. For no breadth was there that intersected my uplifting. The torch of my tension burnt unflickering to the zenith; undiverted, the lightning of the heights hurled down on my head, and earthly fire mixed itself with heavenly fire. The scaffolding of directions had caved in; I, the one set upright, was alone with my direction. And at that time the grace appeared to me which makes one who is borne into one who bears.

Why do we feel ourselves helpless since the might of our life is still confirmed with immortal seals? . . . Do you still know that evening over the sea?

THE WOMAN: Our room hung over the sea. The shore could not be seen. When one looked out, one stood over the water, yes, one stood in the air over the water like a sea gull in turning, like a spirit which hovering pauses and looks. I leaned on the open window in the evening . . .

DANIEL: You leaned on the open window in the evening; the small waves of the sea played against you, and you felt the small waves of your blood in unison with them, felt a mild melancholy and all security. Then you took your eyes away for a moment, you lowered them again half involuntarily, then the world was transformed: instead of the familiar playing of the waves the heavy flood of the night with the horror of its thousand despairings swelled up toward you, and you, who even now were the mistress, felt yourself lost. But then you gazed at the night, as before the sea; with glance and blood you made it into a partner; you tore out of the infinity of its directions the one, that which was yours, and you flung it as a bridge out of the core of your being into the core of the night. Then the horror disappeared; the great being turned its gaze upon you, and the sadness in it was to you, its kindred spirit, no more terrifying than the sadness in the eyes of your dog.

The infinite direction, the infinite tension, the infinite feelings mislead us, cause us to waver, deprive us of our rights. Then I set my inborn direction between them so that they distribute themselves around it as the mysteries of the night around the thrusting line of your glance, like the rock shapes here around the vertical of my body and my climbing step. The clouds of infinity, the waves that go between every pair of the numberless poles of the existent, confused my way; their number is infinite, and my way is one, like my direction. Nonetheless, their multiplicity is only the horizontal which intersects my vertical and I lifted their confusion from my life like the crossbeam from the cross. And that which bore me, now I bear it: as I bear my body.

THE WOMAN: Were we not speaking just now of space? And now it is as if the words that you say are leading us into the spaceless.

DANIEL: The words that *we* are saying. For is not your voice, when you are silent, the guest at my talking? . . . But already when we speak of space, we speak, in fact, of more than space. See, as the manifold sleep is set before the simple awakening, as the manifold horizontal before the simple vertical, so is the manifold Other set before the simple One, before the experience of connection.

THE WOMAN: But is not the manifold the mother, the simple the son?

DANIEL: Perhaps, but you do not come to the mother except through the son—when you go another way, you get lost. Since we cannot live without direction like eternal beings, there remains for us in the eternal only a single way: our direction. Not over the things, not around the things, not between the things—in each thing, in the experience of each thing, the gate of the One opens to you if you bring with you the magic that unlocks it: the perfection of your direction.

THE WOMAN: You forget the power!

DANIEL: No, for direction is only perfect when it is fulfilled with power: the power to live the whole event. Power alone would give you only the fullness, direction alone only the meaning of the life-experience; power and direction together allow you to penetrate into its sub-stance, that is into the unity itself. Thus you find what is sought in vain in the track of the connections.

Look at this stone pine. You may compare its properties with those of other stone pines, other trees, other plants, establish what it has in common and what it does not have in common, explore what it is composed of and how it grew. That will be useful to you in the useful aux-iliary world of names and classifications, of reports about how things arose and how they evolved. You experience nothing of the truth of this being. And now seek to draw near to this stone pine itself. Not with the power of the feeling glance alone—that can present you only with the fullness of an image: much, but not all. Not with the direction of received spirit alone—that can reveal to you only meaning of a living form: much but not all. Rather, with all your directed power, receive the tree, surrender yourself to it. Until you feel its bark as your skin and the springing forth of a branch from the trunk like the striv-ing in your muscles; until your feet cleave and grope like roots and your skull arches itself like a light-heavy crown; until you recognize your children in the soft blue cones; yes, truly until you are transformed. But also in the transformation your direction is with you, and through it you experience the tree so that you attain in it the unity. For it draws you back into yourself; the transformation clears away like a fog; and around your direction a being forms itself, the tree, so that you experience its unity, the unity. Already it is transplanted out of the earth of space into the earth of the soul, already it tells its secret to your heart, already you perceive the mystery of the real. Was it not just a tree among trees? But now it has become the tree of eternal life.

THE WOMAN: But what about when the connection is not the ingeniously spun net of world-knowledge, but the deep element itself: the mother's lap in which we save ourselves from the cruel laws of isolation, the boundless into which we must dive from the shore of limits in order not to perish in contradiction? Is not all ecstasy a merging into the Other?

DANIEL: It was said of Dionysus as Zagreus that the Titans enticed him by means of a game and tore him in pieces and devoured him. He who surrenders himself to ecstasy with undirected soul experiences this fate. The forces of chaos ravish him; the demonia of the unbecome explodes, dismembers his soul, and swallows it. In contrast, I might set the image of Orpheus who descended into the land of Hades with a lyre not in order to regain a beloved but in order to die and rise from the dead with Dionysus, who is Hades, completing the action of renewal in which that rhythm of breathing and of sleep is transfigured into sacrament. But this is the archetypal in Orpheus, that he enters into ecstatic death with the lyre. Not enticed: decided, and with the lyre.

Music is the pure word of the directed soul. Here is nothing more of the ingenious connection out of chained polarities into which the life-experiences are wedged and confined, but also the formless mixture and its lostness are banned from this kingdom. The directed soul alone rules here. It sets its inborn direction, sets the melody in the abyss, and the forces of the deep arrange themselves around it as the "wild beasts" around the playing Orpheus. . . . You come to the mother not otherwise than through the son.

THE WOMAN: So direction is then the inner song?

DANIEL: That the Orphic, the decided, the submerging and anew homecoming, the dying and becoming soul of magic has its song which it keeps intact, immortal in all death—that is the work of its direction. Yes, direction is itself altogether nothing else than magic.

A soul meets the shore of the world. Immediately the whirlpool of happenings plunges over it like an endless sandstorm that threatens to destroy it. It braces itself to withstand it. And see, therein is decided of what nature

a soul is: how it withstands the whirlpool. The one
thinks only of protection. It surrenders itself entirely to
the inherited powers, the traditional arts of self-defense
which educate its senses to perceive in place of the whirlpool an ordered world conceived within the framework
of basic principles of experience. And indeed this *is* protection. For to the benumbed soul the divine force of the
whirlpool is also benumbed. Not so the other. It finds no
satisfaction in the protection that the inherited powers
accord it. It lets it stand, to be sure, the auxiliary world
in which alone it can live with men; it accepts it and
learns its laws. But deep within it grows and endures the
readiness to go out to meet the naked whirlpool. Armed
with what? With nothing other than with the magic of
its direction, its own, inborn, unique direction, belonging
to it and no other. And now I may indeed encompass it
in a verbal definition without having to fear that I shall
injure your conception: Direction is that primal tension
of a human soul which moves it to choose and realize
this and no other out of the infinity of possibilities.
Thus the soul strips off the net of directions, the net of
space and of time, of causes and of ends, of subjects and
of objects; it strips off the net of directions and takes
nothing with it but the magic of its direction. That is
the strength that the soul has found in itself, to which it
recalls itself, which it raises out of itself. And see, dear,
now the power of the directed soul proves itself. For the
directionless god or demon, who does not need direction, may perhaps be blissful, and it is beautiful to think
of him, breathing without direction, circling without

direction, a directionless joy; but wretched is the undirected man who needs direction and must do without
it, the powerless one. Powerful, however, is the directed
soul, since it goes forth to meet the whirlpool, enters into
the whirlpool. And such is its power that it charms it,
magically charms it, so that it stands naked in the naked
and is not destroyed. Rather it rests around the soul, as
the sheath around the sword, as the earth around the
grain of corn, as the mother around the child. And then
the soul knows its mother's lap.

When man had succeeded in harnessing the happening
in the machinery of cause and effect, when the machinery stood joined fast and the skillfully finished clockwork
did its bidden service, then they named the swing of the
pendulum irresistible necessity, and they were horrified
by the necessity. To neither the joinings of human need
between birth and the grave, however, nor to the fate of
all life that is scattered abroad in the world, nor to all
the counterplay of the elements, nor even to the movement of the stars themselves, not to all these investigated
and registered things may I grant the name of necessity,
but only to the directed soul. For as the needle of the
magnet has chosen from all the points of the compass
the north, and as my body has chosen from all positions
the vertical, so the soul from the beginning has chosen
its direction out of the fullness of the all-possible. But
the magnet needle obeys, and each must point to the
same; and even my body obeys and may only carry out in
tension and consciousness what is bidden to all human

bodies. The soul, in contrast, commands and has chosen not obeying but commanding, and it does not know where north is; rather its north is there where it points, and where it points there from eternity to eternity no other can point. And what the ages of the human race could do: to erect a structure of direction whereon nature regulates itself for the human senses, that the soul can surpass; for with its one direction it summons reality and conjures it, conjures it around its direction, so that the reality does not regulate but reveals and delivers itself, not to the senses and the understanding alone but from being to being and from mother to child. Thus the directed soul is the necessity of nature.

But direction is the necessity of the soul. And because my body is happy with my soul since its direction mirrors itself in your direction, I might here, standing between the rocks, sing a prize song to you, if I could do it properly. But, in fact, it can only be said in deeds, not in words, and it manifests itself only through its effect: it is that which pulls me up in the morning and drives me into the wilderness, which visits me at midday and sends me to the living, which takes my hand at evening and leads me to God—the high mistress of my all-solitude.

THE WOMAN: . . . Give me your hand, Daniel.

DANIEL: Here.

THE WOMAN: . . . What do you see?

DANIEL: My hand in yours.

THE WOMAN: A horizontal, is it not?

DANIEL: A horizontal.

THE WOMAN: Might you—might you remove the crossbeams?

DANIEL: For nothing.

THE WOMAN: How so?

DANIEL: Because this is not the compulsion by the other which it is valid to overcome, but the choice of the other: the direction of the holy spirit, the flowering cross of community.

II

On Reality

Dialogue above the City

ULRICH: How the voices of the city die away! Only
in this small stretch have we wandered from them, and
already all their noise, which even now spurted up to us,
has fallen into the great mixing bowl of distance, and of
all the storms of its haste this rustle remains with us—
almost a song.

DANIEL: A song, Ulrich, a song! Yes, they tugged and
shrieked like sick hounds on the chain, the goal-possessed
thousand-times-thousand; they raged against and through
one another, and still there throbbed unknown in each
throat the longing for the song that is liberated now
not in their ears but in ours. There was a moment when
I heard it otherwise: in the midst of the tumult of the
street, not a play of the distance, but the bleeding near-
ness, sung to me by the longing of the longing ones.

ULRICH: *One* moment?

DANIEL: Do you not know what the moment which
you allow to fulfill itself brings to you, what a flood of

song and light? . . . I went among the crowd and thought
of nothing other than opening my soul so wide to it, so
to unbolt granary and treasure house that everything
might find place in it of that open and hidden need
of these men of which I could in any way be aware. I
spoke within myself: What can I do for you, you who
rush around me without purpose and touch me without
understanding, nameless crowd? I have not the power
to heal you and have not the art to comfort you; and
if I sacrificed my life for you, nothing would be accom-
plished. But this I may do: receive you, gather your
scattered pain in me, make your torn pieces whole in
me, so that my soul may become your song, you song-
less one. And with this will I went through the crowd.
And then this will became actual in me; it happened to
me, so that I no longer knew myself but only a tumult
of forces, hitting and rushing past one another without measure or way. But in the center of the tumult a
heart dwelt, like a human heart, which received blood
from the whirl and sent it again to all its corners. And
the presence of this formless and unruly body at first
so overpowered me that I performed my service like a
pump, humble and stupefied. But then meaning came
over me again, and I received from each of these forces,
yes, from each of these galloping, purpose-mad forces—
from the hungry and the greedy, from the seeking and
the grasping—rising from each, I received a song. O
that pale, flickering, ghostlike singing! As I received
it, I became fainthearted, my friend, fainthearted with
choking compassion, and no longer had any will in me

other than this one—to be again a man and to take one
of these men by the hand and say to him: "Remember,
brother, that your soul is a free and mighty firmament
that nothing can compel." Then I threw off and abjured
my office, and already I stood again in my body, in the
midst of the crowd. But I did so trembling and saw what
was around me as a gigantic circling top, and my lips
were struck dumb. Thus I stood trembling and mute,
and after I had stood awhile, I went home and sat on
a bench in the garden on the brown bench under the
maple tree and was alone in a worse loneliness than
ever before . . .

Only much later, however, was it revealed to me what I
had known in that moment.

ULRICH: In that moment? How can you be so certain of
that?

DANIEL: You know certainly about what is called the
sign in an act of knowing. You wake up one morning
or you pause on a walk and you have a thought in your
hands, a knowing thought that you see for the first time
and yet which is as ripe and ready as if you had formed it
over a very long time. But while you are regarding it, you
notice that it bears a sign: it is an image out of a place
and a moment and in it the seal of a life-experience. And
whether you establish your knowledge in the holiness of
a silence or offer it for sale on the market of words, the
sign cleaves to it.

ULRICH: And perhaps it is this that allows us to feel our knowledge as something living and indestructible even when it is preserved in silence. . . . But what was it, Daniel, that you knew at that time?

DANIEL: If I may say it to you as simply as I knew it: he remains unreal who does not realize.

ULRICH: You will probably have to say it to me more complexly if I am to understand it.

DANIEL: Indeed, we already spoke once of the fact that there is a twofold relation of man to his experience: the orienting or classifying and the realizing or making real. What you experience, doing and suffering, creating and enjoying, you can register in the structure of experience for the sake of your aims or you can grasp it for its own sake in its own power and splendor. In so far as you fit it into the experience, you elaborate it according to the forms and laws of experience. It no more occupied a space than the new heaven which John saw at Patmos; but you make it into a thing in space, fix it in its place with the cipher of a column of air above it and the cipher of the earth's gravity below it, with an unshakably fixed relationship to each other point of the world. It was no more temporal than the last, already double-directed glance of the dying man; you make it into an event in time, expand it into a sequence, as a boy violently spreads out a rosebud, and then you shove it between a before and an after which squash it flat. It was no more causal than the majesty of the first dream; you force it into a chain where it represents just as much meaning as every other link in the chain: joining it as a link with another link. It was no more an object than God is an object to man or man to God: you break it in two so that you injure its core and with superior certainty name the pieces the perceiving and the perceived. But when it has been inserted in these and similar structures and machineries, so that the inserted parts fit with one another and it may be found in them again at any time, and when the sketch of insertions can be expressed in a generally understandable statement, then this statement is commonly called the truth. And to a certain extent rightly so; for doubt is at home on journeys of discovery, but truth and error are easily established in reading a map. Only one shall not speak of reality in all this.

ULRICH: Why, Daniel? Do you wish to assert that science, which is verified in natural happenings and in purposeful acts, is not built throughout on reality?

DANIEL: I do indeed mean that. But understand me rightly. The structure of experience appears to me ingenious but not artificial; it seems to me an elaboration of life-experience, yet not an arbitrary one. It has still drawn all its forms and laws, yes its whole existence, determined by ancient goals, out of nothing other than precisely the eternal life-experience of man, and what it has established in regularities reflects deep rhythmic traits of life-experience, to be sure only symbolically.

And how should I not honor this unsurveyable edifice
of science and its wonderful development? How could I
wish it away, wish to go back behind it, without trans-
gressing against the power of the spirit? For everywhere
where a knowing was formed, where it began, where it
was creative, it was not orienting but realizing; immer-
sion in pure life-experience, and what was thus found
was carried over into the bed of enregistering. And
everywhere where orienting knowledge ruled autono-
mously it was robbery, for it took place at the cost of the
mothering, nourishing juices of life-experience and was
only able to transpose the realization in the greater into
a little need or a little security. And it is this predominance of the orienting from which I suffer and against
which I rebel—for the sake of the realizing which creates
out of the life-experience of reality.

ULRICH: Then you want to understand by reality not
the elementary material of the life-experience but a work
of the soul?

DANIEL: A work of the soul certainly; but consider
that in life-experience we are not offered a material that
we form and that is detachable for our forming, extract-
able out of it; rather that it sprouts in our activity and
that in the finished plant we can no longer in any way
separate out the seed. Life-experience is only given to
us to observe and compare in the form which our function, orienting or realizing, has developed out of it; in
its unformed essence we only experience it, but we do

not possess it. To our knowledge, to our memory, to our taking possession of it there lead from experience only the two bridges of our formation, and when it has crossed the bridge—even though its passage were faster than the speed of light—it is formed; it has become mere experience or reality. Life-experience is ungraspable like a lightning flash or a waterfall or the formation of crystals; we may not call it reality since we cannot thereby deal with it, draw it forth, and regard it. But still less will we accord the name of reality to the superstructure of experience.

ULRICH: But what do you think about the common usage of speech to which reality is simply the totality of the perceived and the perceivable which is experienced as the existing?

DANIEL: It seems to me that we should pay attention to it because the life of men together is erected upon it, and not only for that reason. And we shall accept it again as soon as we have returned into the enclosure of the city, with a qualification, if that seems good to you, or unqualified. But now . . . has it not often struck you that in a poem, Hölderlin's perhaps, a word is employed in a heightened meaning that the common usage does not know?

ULRICH: In a poem certainly.

DANIEL: And are not poems soaring knowledge? So let us now linger in a poem and call that reality which is to

be called reality in a heightened meaning. And be sure
that this heightened meaning, to which we now want
to attend for a while, is even so little arbitrariness as
the heightened meaning of the word in poetry. But this
arises out of a no less deep necessity and a deeper legiti-
macy than the customary usage, which indeed corrobo-
rates the heightened meaning by subordinating itself to
the poet after decades or centuries and adapting itself to
his meaning. Why so? Because that heightened meaning
stems from moments of heightened existence, heightened
humanity, heightened knowledge. It is these that fix
speech, renew speech. They must be taken into consideration when we wish to talk of reality and realization in a
heightened, in a creative sense.

ULRICH: But how can we take them into consideration
when they are inaccessible to us?

DANIEL: Not more inaccessible than the hero is to the
poet who knows him only because, having met with his
face and his gesture in the world, he finds present in his
soul what is expressed in this face and gesture . . .

Picture to yourself a man who remembers. I do not mean
that resigned laziness which leaves the doors of the past
open and turns to every entering shadow the same bit-
tersweet attentiveness; also not that assumed superiority
that reckons up what has been like the earlier moves of
a game in which the decisive is still to be done; but also
not that true and thankful accounting of a true man

who judges the decisions and the absences of decision of his life. I mean the rarest of all, the heightened hour of great evocation when his lived life steps up to the testifying man like a form. See him, possessed by the shudder of the event, of the whole of which he has only now become fully aware; see him compose himself, govern his glance, behold. The image that he beholds is woven out of nothing else than out of that mysterious material that we call time, lived time. Out of the faces of lived time the holy countenance is unfolded, and the beholder recognizes this image which continually changes according to the meaning of life. What times, do you think, will he see again thus? Those in which he inserts his life-experience in the inherited structure of mediacy as a servant of the alien? Or those in which he catches them, as the ballplayer the ball, hurling himself against them, receiving them with hastily collected limbs; in which he embraces them, as the wrestler embraces the body tensed against him, throwing his whole strength into a muscle struggling for victory; in which he completes it as the runner his course, fulfilling, completing it with the swing of his own stride? Which, which does he recognize as reality, the hours in which the many overshadow and weaken the one or those in which the one shines in the undiminished fullness of its splendor because it is related to nothing other than to itself?

Yes, this is what it means to realize: to relate life-experience to nothing else but itself. And here is the place where the power of the human spirit awakens and collects itself and becomes creative. For where orientation rules, that crafty economy is at home whose shrewdness stinks to heaven because it only saves and never renews. But where the foot of realization stands, there power is drawn from the depths and collected and moved to action and renewed in work. As the ballplayer and the wrestler and the runner each is summoned by his task to draw all the force out of his body and pour it into the act, so life-experience calls to the man who is ready to realize it. For he may do that only as a whole and united person. And he who had only to register in the system of experiencing, and living with only one part of his being, could come to terms with the all, must now bring forth the totality of his being in order to withstand a single thing or event. But because the power gives itself in this way to the one thing, it becomes creative in it, creates reality in it, through it. For that alone is reality which is so lived. And all effective reality of the human world is lived thus, has been created thus.

ULRICH: Then it is so that what we call creating is only the expression of realizing? And the creative man is the realizing one?

DANIEL: It is tempting, Ulrich, when one has recognized two forces of the soul as different, now also to construct two different classes of men and to lend to the first the one, to the second the other as their fixed and exclusive primal properties. But I can only imagine a creative man as one in whom that genuine iron ore that every,

even the most miserable, human soul conceals becomes
steel at red and then at white heat; only one in whom
the spirit that is common to all fulfills itself unchecked
in effective consequence. And in him as in all, the living
encamps near the dead, only that in him the sunlike
might of what is living makes what is dead fall into dust
as we look at it. In him as in everybody, the growing
borders on the stifled, the free on the warped, wisdom on
folly—only that which lives with us counts for nothing
else when the steel of genius flashes up into the air and
strikes its blows. And so, a realizing kind of man, an
orienting kind of man also do not exist. A purely realizing man would disappear in God; a purely orienting
man degenerate into nothingness. Rather realization
and orientation dwell close together, like conception and
pregnancy, like knowledge and dissemination, like discovery and utilization. As in the life of the community
the attained reality must ever again be inserted in the
structure of experience, so in the life of the individual,
hours of inserting follow hours of realization and must so
follow; the solitary reality is still not only the highest of
blisses but also the heaviest of burdens.

But in this you speak truly, that the name creative
man belongs to him who has the most effective power
of realization, to him in whom the realizing power of
the soul has so concentrated into work that it creates
reality for all. His realizing hours unite into a succession
of summits of the eternal which shine forth out of the
fleeting series of ups and down of his human life; even in

his orienting the impulse of the actual lives on. For what belongs to man as a species before he lets himself be overrun by his aims, to primitive man, and what belongs to each individual man before he lets himself be overrun by his aims, that belongs to the creative man: the unbroken power of realization. But this power is strong in the primitive man and the child only because the orienting ability has not matured enough to be able to consume it; in creativity, in contrast, mature orientation is also included, but as a dependent and serving function. The primitive man and the child are *still*, the creative man *newly* master of reality. A moonbeam lies on the forehead of the former like a mirroring of a forgotten paradise, but the latter shines with the fire that it has stolen from heaven. They dream reality; it awakens it, the vigilant watchtower warder of the earth. And therefore the inner meaning of realization is revealed to him as to no other: that the realizing man is the genuinely real. For as the things that stand in his life-experiencing become reality, so also he himself.

ULRICH: But the things are still only real for the realizing man; for whom is he real?

DANIEL: It would be very much preferable if we did not assert that the things are real "for him." Is the fire there for the iron or the iron for the fire or both only for the smith? No matter, the steel really comes forth and works. Realizing life-experience creates the essential form of existence of which we speak. What we call things and what we call I are both comprehended in what is thus created; both find their reality here; both can only find it here. For all life-experiencing is a dream of unification; orientation divides and sunders it, realization accomplishes and proclaims it. Thus all reality is fulfilled unification. Nothing individual is real in itself; everything individual is only preparation. The creative hours, acting and beholding, forming and thinking, are the unifying hours. The unifying person is the hero and the sage, the poet and the prophet; communion names his mystery, and he is real because he shares in its reality, because in the times of intensity is a real part. A something is not real for him, but with him; out of his life-experiencing, reality ascends that encompasses him. Reality for whom? For all, because out of it a seed of realizing falls in all? For a self that experiences us and receives from us nothing other than our reality? For no one? It does not matter: it *is*, and is not less if it is beheld by no eyes.

ULRICH: Then the creative man is thus a separate and select man?

DANIEL: Only in the sense that in him there appears concentrated and effectively real what is sketched in all. In each man there dwells, utilized or suppressed, the power to become unified and to enter into reality. Yes, there are many, silent and unknown, who are equal to the creative in realizing power and yet do not reveal it in the world, whether because they lack the desire and art of far-reaching expression, because out of respect for the grace that has descended upon them they choose a life in a narrow circle and only become visible to what is near them, or because they are turned away and consecrated (for even the true hermit cannot persist without realizing power). These we may inscribe as the nameless on the tablet upon which the names of the creative stand—for the sake of their reality, because reality is splendid even when we only have a hint of it, but also for the sake of their effect, for the paths of effectiveness are a mystery, and it is often revealed to us in all stillness that the deeds of the secret ones are greater than the deeds of those who are in vogue.

ULRICH: Do you not think, too, Daniel, that those of whom you speak are few in our time?

DANIEL: Realizing men are few in our time. It is busy replacing them by the producers.

ULRICH: The producers? Whom do you call by this name?

DANIEL: Those who work without being, who give what they do not possess, who triumph where they have not fought: the pet children of appearance. They shun realization from of old or have renounced it when they take leave of their youth. But they do or make things such as once came only out of realization, or at least deceptively similar things. They do or make them brightly and with elegance; they do not demand, as realization did, that others join in their doing; they are satisfied that one recognizes them; how could one deprive oneself of them? God once created the world in six days, but since then we have learned the technique of creation. With its help the apes of God make the world in one day, and it is more interesting.

ULRICH: Why so bitter, Daniel? Let them be!

DANIEL: Shall I not be bitter against the signature of this age? Do you not know the king who has installed these satraps? He is the same one who has stifled the power of realization in the bands of contemporary men. It is inborn in all of them in some strength, with some drive; and in all of them it does not attain to its height, and is hemmed in and destroyed and degraded. But the fact is that the power of realization cannot be injured by any earthly need or necessity; the only force which can attack and oppress it is the predominance of orientation. And that is the predominance that has insinuated itself into the blood of our age and dissolved its reality in order to put in its place its own brood, appearance. For before all other ages of civilization ours is the age that does not realize.

Look at this city that rushes along beneath us. Now dissolve also the contours of its image, and it lies under the veil of the evening distance as if it slept. But even in its sleep the fever of its days does not forsake it, and its dreams are like wanderings in the wilderness. Look, look through the veil: how beautiful it is, how strong, and how sick. For it has fallen to appearance.

The city, we say, but we do not, in fact, mean its houses and its factories, its wares and its refuse; we mean, in fact, these millions of men—not a number, Ulrich, forget the number, not a crowd, break up the crowd—all these individual men, naked underneath their clothes, bleeding under their skin, all these whose uncovered heartbeat united would drown out the united voice of their machines. These men are wronged, Ulrich, wronged in the right of rights, the gracious right of reality.

They have aims, and they know how to attain them. They have an environment, and they have information about their environment. They also have spirituality of many kinds, and they talk a great deal. And all of this outside of the real. They live, and they do not realize what they live. Their experience is ordered without being comprehended. They experience of it what component part it has in common with other experiences, and are oriented. To each of them eternity calls, "Be!" They smile at eternity and answer, "I have information." Their limitation is so closely cut to the body that they are glad and proud of it, and call it by elegant and pretentious names, such as culture, or religion, or progress, or tradition, or intellectuality: Ah, the unreal has a thousand masks.

Orientation is their lord—the spherical monistic or the conical theological or even only the waltz of the practical empiricism which helps in every need and removes all trouble. In the dead light of orientation, their destiny, which was summoned to experience living illumination in a living way and to become illuminated in itself, passes away. They walk as unreal men, hunt, storm after their aims. And, like the fiery columns of an evil demiurge, the aims stride before them and dupe them: but they plunge after, running and sliding past one another like an anarchic dance of specters.

ULRICH: But is our age really the only one so constituted? Were there not many before it?

DANIEL: No age of history, Ulrich, could escape the leveling power of orientation, the registering, the utilizing. But always the great multitude of realizing men stood in their midst and dispensed warmth, movement, self-activity. The *terra incognita* was always beheld before it was measured, named, and unregistered. And even though man was long since overwhelmed by the ghosts of his aims and surrounded by the gigantic, in realization he had a dimension before whose threshold they remained standing and waited for the command of the wonderful wanderer. But an age came which succumbed to the superabundance of its material. That was the age when the aims themselves were surrounded by the means, numberless gnomes, each one of which now behaved like a tiny aim. And the soul stood opposite this swarming world of means, had to find its way in it, assert itself, protect its security. How could that take place?

Through realization which, as one knew well, was full of insecurity and danger, profound and without safeguard? Could this infinitely developed life be mastered only on the strenuous, time- and strength-consuming detour of realization? Must this not be achieved more directly and without danger by orientation alone? They celebrated the great triumph of the investigation of nature in that they attributed to themselves the victory of realization, as the seneschal in the fairy tale replaced the sleeping dragon slayer. And thus the sin against the spirit took place, innocently and unforgivably.

Spirit is realization: unity of the soul, exclusiveness of life-experience, unification. But these men are yoked in the multiplicity of their aims, their means, their knowledge—everything is conditioned by everything, everything is decided out of everything, everything is related to everything, and over all there rules the security of orientation that has information. Yes, they have escaped the dangers of the deep. Concentrate oneself in life-experience? They concentrate in their work only their strength to work, and it succeeds; and their satisfaction means dispersion. Comprehend the life-experience in itself? If they could hunt up its contents on their map of heaven and earth, with names, neighborhood, length and breadth! Become united with a reality? They know that in this world one gets further by dissecting than by unifying, and what is needed by way of unification is taken care of at the same time by the competent retorts of orientation.

ULRICH: As much as I agree with you, there seems to me much that is immoderate in what you say, as though you meant all of the men of this city, and yet you know many and surely have an intimation of several who . . .

DANIEL: Am I Yahweh and hold the punishing fire in my hands that I should enumerate the righteous? Or will it be pleasant to me to bear them in mind when this city is smitten with unreality? For the city, for the crowd, for the wretched millions my heart swells and revolts.

The unreal, the wretched! If my arm could only immerse them in the fire of renewal and baptize them to a second birth! If my mouth could only awaken the song the longing for which throbs unknown in each of these throats! If I could only redeem these specters to reality!

ULRICH: And do you think that the need and the contradiction, the wrong and the madness of the age when it is genuinely lived will become reality? That then all, as today the few, will know the great horror and the great compassion? That the flood of reality will tear down the dams of theories, of programs, of parties, and shake the innermost souls? That the realizing man must first of all realize the chaos?

DANIEL: Yes, Ulrich! And only thus could he begin, begin again. For in the world of mankind there is no other beginning than reality.

ULRICH: Begin again, Daniel? Then we shall go back behind what this strange age, despite all its greatness, has given?

DANIEL: No, rather all that must be genuinely conquered for reality in new, unheard-of battle. What now has its spectral existence in the deceptive game of unholy haste, in the distorted mirror of aims, in the illusory structure of information and false security, that shall—that must—Ulrich, become real, lived life. And that is life of immediacy and of human fellowship; for in genuine community as in genuine solitude it is immediacy which alone makes it possible to live the realizing as real.

III

On Meaning

Dialogue in the Garden

DANIEL: Quick and young as the unexpected stride,
I heard your stride along my garden wall, and you did,
indeed, come unexpectedly, Reinold. Never before have
you visited me in the morning. You are welcome; I could
only say that to a few at this hour. For how many friends
might stand in the face of the awakening garden? The
trees condemn him who is not upright and attentive; the
flowers judge him who does not open himself and submit
himself to the sun; and he who does not know the peace
of becoming, against him every blade of grass raises itself
like a flaming sword.

REINOLD: You praise me for the first time, Daniel. I
have often thought of how it would be if you praised me
once, and how I should be glad of it. And now you praise
me, and so much, and I cannot be glad. For I know that I
do not stand before your garden. The peace of becoming,
you say—I no longer know any calm. Rather restlessness and wandering and the worst anxiety—these have
become my comrades.

DANIEL: How has this happened to you, Reinold? For that this is something foreign to you, you also feel even now.

REINOLD: O that I could only confess it to you. I have come in order to speak with you about it, but now that I am here I am ashamed. When I was a child, I once came running to my mother and called to her that I had caught a fish. She looked up at me, and I saw only then that she sat at the weaving loom. Then my beautiful fish became entirely insignificant to me before the mystery of the appearing and disappearing threads—and as often as I recalled that since then, I had to be ashamed.

DANIEL: Just speak, you do right in doing so. So long as one is in the calm of his becoming, the Thou that he bears in himself may be enough for him. But when the flood comes to him, then his need and summons is to find the Thou to whom he can speak in the world.

REINOLD: You read to us once a Celtic song; in it were a pair of verses that struck me as though I had long known and forgotten them:

> You do not tarry long wandering
> In the land with the living heart.

That was my childhood, Daniel: the land with the living heart. As the warm body has its heart that collects and distributes all the blood, and here the movement

of the saps is set by center and unity, so the life of the
child had a heart: it had an inexpressible, inexpress-
ibly real meaning which was center and unity for it.
A meaning, Daniel, one single, own meaning. And
you must know that I was not at all lost in reverie, as
other children probably are; and still the meaning was
with me. It came just from nowhere, it was there, and I
felt it as one feels his heart: there you are, deep-rooted
in me, familiar, adventurous, small secret sun of this
wonderful world! Meaning, meaning—the falling stars
of the August nights had it not more and not less than
the cut-off hair that I saw fall down on me; the narrow,
immeasurable horizon of my space and my time was
golden-rimmed with meaning. Nothing meaningless
happened to me. When I awakened out of the music
of my dreams into the dark, the night had my mother's
arms and even motherly words like hers, and when a
heavy illness befell me, the otherwise invisible ones
were with me as guests and the plane on which I had
lived rounded itself for me to a sphere.

And the things, the things, Daniel: the concaveness
of the things was in my senses; the things clung close
within it as the peach in the hollow of the hand. All
beings and all events were in accord, more and otherwise
than an account balances, more and otherwise than
a song harmonizes; everything was attuned with me,
everything concurred, everything was in accord out of
its united self. Life did not at all appear to me peaceable
and accommodating because of that; but hardness and

sharpness, conflict and misfortune were like the fixed moves in a game that includes all kinds of moves in its rules and precisely thereby is meaningful.

So I was secure, Daniel, at ten years, at twelve years, at sixteen years, securer in the world than when I drank my mother's milk; at ten years, at twelve years, at sixteen years, secure with the security of the ruling one. And I stepped out of my childhood without stepping out of my security. I learned to know the overly bright duality of life, enmity and love, and the *meaning* did not fade for me. Out of my world, not out of a strange one came the enemy toward me, came woman toward me, and he was not the opponent, she was not the temptress, but both joined with me in arteries and veins which flowed into that heart, the meaning. And I was not soft to the one, not comfortable with the other, but in the midst of anger and longing both were primally and eternally familiar. Thus my eighteenth, my twentieth, my twenty-third year streamed and rested in the security of being in harmony and ruling. I was no longer a child, but around me there played at every hour a happy child, my sister, the world; and as long as she was near me and I was turned to her, nothing could harm me.

Someone other than you might ask me what has "happened" since then. But you once said to us that the decisions dwell not in the rise but in the dip of the folds, and so you will understand me.

This spring on my journey home out of the south I came one evening to Spezia. I had wanted to travel on throughout the night, but the sight of the sea was so powerful that it foolishly struck me to want it despite my intention. I descended, went to the harbor, took a small boat and rowed out. It was a new moon, but from the depths above me a chorus of southern stars sang down on me; my oar cut dark flood and concealed splendor; boundlessness was the bed of my soul, heaven, night, and sea its cushion. It was one of the hours in which we no longer know more strongly what we do than what is done about us and with us. So as I now turned the boat and returned to the shore, I was barely conscious of the action of my hands.

Now I looked up casually—and was terrified. Everything that I had just now possessed had disappeared. Out of a dumb infinity an army of jack-o'-lanterns stared into empty infinity; threateningly, thousands of moist lips, sneering cruelly, opened and closed about me, and in the nape of my neck, dark and tangible as a betrayal, the presence of the night beings grew. Where the bed of my soul had been, was the nothing; seduced, betrayed, re-jected, my soul hung in the grey of the night between sea and heaven. I did not understand, but I steeled myself for battle: "I am there, I am there," I cried, "and you cannot annihilate me," and strength spurted into my shoulders and my legs at the same time, and gripped, with the feet firmly planted and the oars out: to the shore!

Then a shrill conflict of light swept over a piece of the
shore and tore it loose. Shamelessly it stood stretched
out from out of the darkness and bellowed the nonsense
of its clarity out over the flood. Clarity—but I did not
recognize it; bold and strange it sprang out of the night
as out of a black house door. And already the night swal-
lowed it again; and for a moment I could compose myself
and *knew* all: the approaching storm and the cruiser over
yonder that was using its searchlights. But when immediately thereafter the cold lightning bit into the land,
my knowledge was of no use to me. Spectral stretches
of earth detached themselves from one another before
me in a senseless service; not like parts of a shore, but
like spectral shrieks. I "knew" that they were connected,
a busy and friendly little land, and knew the hearty
smacks of the fishermen's children in their cradles and
the stamping of the sailor's hornpipe in the tavern; but I
felt no connection, rather shriek, shriek, and in between
them the abyss.

The abyss was between piece and piece of the world,
between thing and thing, between image and being,
between the world and me—when the light of the
searchlight came. And the feet firmly planted, with
working arms, rowing to the known shore, surrounded
by the shrill of the spectral truth, I longed for comfort like the dying Christ for the communion, and my
benumbed soul longed for its sacrament, for *meaning*: for
the meaning had burst, a bloody tear ran right through
the middle of it. And I saw the ultimate: in me, in my

inmost self, was the abyss. I was forever divided; not into
spirit and body, as joined and detached in each other as
ever, but in the thousandfold, Protean doubleness of the
bright One and the dark Other, with the eternal abyss
in between. There my last security shattered; broken I
set foot on the shore, and when I set foot on the shore,
it was to me a discordant, disjointed life. Behind me the
storm rose over the sea, before me lay the calm land; but
it was to me as though I now left the last, fearful hiding
place of calm and entered into the harsh storm that
would never end.

Since then the abyss is before me at all times—the
nameless that everything that is named proclaims.

And it is strange, Daniel: when I had security, men
appeared to me at times insecure in their questions and
doubts; but now that I have lost my ground, they stand
around me in superior equilibrium, like the sober around
the drunk. And yet they know about the abyss; but they
also have information. And they are not stingy with
their information.

There are the world-knowers. That is the abyss between
the things and the consciousness, they say; and this
abyss is an illusion, for consciousness is a power among
powers, and all is one. But what good does it do me that
they deny what I have experienced with my being? Shall
I subjugate myself to the storm of my knowledge to a
formula, so they examine and reject it? Shall the truth

verify itself to me in a finished agreement, instead of in the totality of my life-experience?

And there are the God-knowers. That is the abyss between man and God, they say; and at a certain place on a certain day it has been filled up for each one who henceforth believes in this filling up. Thus it is not filled up for me; for me it must be filled up here and now since I behold it here and now. Here and now is infinity and eternity like only nowhere and never; and here and now is the abyss. And I should rather behold it on all days and in all dreams and even in the hour of my death than smear my eyes with its salve and become blind to my truth.

And there are the mind-knowers. That is the abyss between the idea and the experience, they say; that is the abyss above which it is our office to build a bridge. And they build bridges out of transparent luster, the most beautiful in the world. But thought alone can set foot on these bridges; under every other step they break down. And it is not, indeed, my thought that beholds the abyss, it is my *being*: this thing made of stone and storm and flood and flame, this whole, weighing down, springing upward—this substance. There it stands, the elemental, and smiles at the beautiful bridges on which its child, thought, may dance.

And there are the knowers of mysteries. That is the abyss between the world of appearance and the true world, they say; we fly over it with our mystery. And truly, they have an airship, a wonderful one built out of sheer mystery; it ascends resoundingly, straight up into the air. It took me with it, and I felt wonderful, as though behind all the heavy seriousness there must still hide only a plaything. And so it was. For when we were again below, they said: Now we are on the other side. That seemed strange to me, for it was all like this side. And when I looked closely, I noticed that we stood on the same spot as before. Then I went my way.

And now I have come to you, Daniel, to learn whether you can tell me what I should do.

DANIEL: Imagine a wanderer who on a deep, cloudy night after long wandering comes into the outermost street of an unknown city. Hour after hour he has walked in the empty darkness of the heath, no presence about him except that of the meager thickets; now he steps into the midst of another darkness, one that is filled to the rim with strange, threatening life. The houses stand like vague monsters with staring eyes and insidiously open jaws; between the houses the unknown extends, and the lights that flicker in the misty foreground are unsteady like the signals of a gang of murderers. No step is in the street, no sound; but its silence seems treacherous and its forsakenness like something lying in wait. Behind the hazy visible, from every quarter in the overfull invisible, danger gathers, slides, waltzes. And in the anxious heart of the wanderer one longing is powerful—for security.

And because he longs for security, he needs above all else this one thing: to know his way about. What sort of a city is this? Where does this street lead? How do I get out of this sinister place? To know one's way about—that is the key to salvation and health, to security itself.

Of such nature is the longing of those who, seized by the shudder of the boundless or by the glimpse of the contradiction, only wish to protect themselves. Their being has become mature for knowledge, the mystery has opened itself to them, but they do not prepare themselves to withstand it. The irrational makes them anxious; instead of *realizing* it, receiving it into life-experience with the whole strength of the moment, they strive only to guard their security. All living with the whole being and with unconstrained force means danger; for there is no thing, no relation, no happening in the world that thus known does not reveal its bottomless abyss, and all thinking threatens to shatter the stability of the knower. But danger is what they wish to avoid; they will not risk their skin for the sake of a vain problematic. They want security, and security once for all. He who lives his life in genuine, realizing knowledge must perpetually begin anew, perpetually risk all anew; and thus his truth is not a having but a becoming. But they want to know where they are; they do not want to be under way but at home; they want to be provided for and insured; want a solid general truth that will not let itself be overturned; want only to know their way about, want only to *orient* themselves in the world, that is, protect themselves in the world. So they build their ark or have it built, and they name the ark *Weltanschauung*,* and seal up with pitch not only its cracks but also its windows. But outside are the waters of the living world.

But set another wanderer in that place and let the same street, the same hour envelop him. He goes, he remains standing, he turns himself, with wide-open senses, with opened spirit, willing and firm. He does not want to know his way about; how could he ever experience of this here more than now and thus? He wants only to live this here—the wild darkness, the fallow, animal faces of the houses and the reeling lights in the depths—so completely that it becomes for him reality and message. Of what value is it to him what city this is? Here it speaks to him in another tongue than in that in which names exist. What does it mean to him where this street leads? Now he is in it, truly in it, and may not be elsewhere. It is not sinister to him; does not the indefinite proclaim existing being just as faithfully as the definite? Does not the insidious attest to the holy power as fervently as the reliable?

He is no less turned to the compressed breath of the lurking than the even breath of the sleeping. He knows danger and will meet it when it is demanded; he has a strong wrist and knows how to defend himself; but

* World view. [Translator]

what would life be if it did not everywhere approach the uttermost and threaten to capsize? The script of life is so unspeakably beautiful to read because death looks over our shoulder.

Such is the way of him who forgets himself in order to practice realization according to his strength. He does not long for the security of knowing his way about, which can only succeed when the life-experience is not lived to its ground, when only the surface is taken from it, that which can be rationalized and ordered; he loves danger and the underived truth which he who ventures draws from the depths. He does not want to know where he is; how could he, for he is not always at the same place but is ever at the new, ever at the uttermost. Ever at God, I may even say, since God cannot, in fact, realize himself in man otherwise than as the innermost presence of a life-experience, and for him therefore it is not the same, but ever the new, the uttermost, the god of this life-experience. Orientation, which acts as the all-embracing, is thoroughly godless; godless also is the theologian who fixes his God in causality, a helping formula of orientation, and the spiritualist who knows his way about in the "true world" and sketches its topography; all religiousness degenerates into religion and church when it begins to orient itself: when instead of the one thing needful it provides a survey of what one must believe in this life and the beyond, and promises having instead of becoming, security instead of danger.

All security which is promised, all security which is longed for and acquired, means to protect oneself. It is that which is promised and allotted to the believers of all old and new churches. But he who loves danger and practices realization does not want to protect himself but to realize himself. He is the unprotected in the world, but he is not abandoned; for there is nothing that can lead him astray. He is not at home in the world, yet he is at home at all times; for the ground of each thing wishes to harbor him. He does not possess the world, yet stands in its love; for he realizes all being in its reality. He knows no security yet is never unsure; for he possesses steadfastly that before which all security appears vain and empty: direction and meaning.

The wanderer who remained standing was not oriented and did not want to be; he did not know the name of the city into which he had entered, what the place was called, where the street led; but when he walked further, his step did not hesitate, and when he came to a crossroad, he chose with immediate decision as out of a deep command. He who has direction does not have information as to how the will is determined in cause and effect, nor as to what one must hold to be good and bad, nor that there is an evolution in which one is imprisoned; but when he acts, he does his deed and no other, he chooses his lot and no other, he decides with his being. The secure man is entangled in the net of his system of orientation; his action stands on its spot in world and

time and has no more space than this spot affords it; it
is limited before and after by evolution, for how could he
trust himself to do that which evolution has not autho-
rized him to do? But he who has direction and practices
realization, to him the deed is not limited by causality
and evolution; he feels himself free and acts as a free
man. Let the orienting man call his freedom the illusion
of subjectivity, let him prove the conditioned nature of
his deed and describe its origin: everything may be presented afterward that is not a part of his reality; all revo-
lution sees that which comes afterward as evolution. But
to him who ever begins anew the deed is as magic is to
the primitive man: as the magic action does not hang in
a chain of happenings but is a world event which begins
and ends out of itself, as there on the path from working
to effecting the whole expresses itself and the ring closes
itself, so he who ever begins anew does the deed out of
itself into being as an act of creation and a completion.
This is direction: the magic power of unconstrained
acting which wants to realize itself and chooses its deed
with the being.

And over it the star shines down *meaning* and sends its
beam into all happening.

The wanderer who remained standing in the outermost
street and did not hesitate at the crossroads, came to
a place around which grew plane trees; he sat down
beneath one of them and looked up at the heavens. At
this moment the clouds parted, and a solitary, very bright

star appeared to the eyes of the man, who greeted it like a brother. "All the time you were turned to me," he said, "and now I *see* you too, distant and friendly one, ever present one!" And in the light of the star all his wanderings timelessly arose for him in great truth, together with the heath and the road and this place between the plane trees, living deeply in its own meaning, as a myth of being and a revelation.

Meaning is not, like the ark of those who protect themselves, constructed out of planks, with joints sealed up with pitch, but is singly created out of the material of the element, like the fiery chariot which carried Elijah away. One cannot scrape it together out of experiences of just any kind, nor does it let itself be taught and transmitted; rather it is joined to the soul as a primal possession, to be unfolded and verified in its life-experience. And as the painter who singly wills the painting still accomplishes the work as an expression of the spirit and as witness of his daimon, so the soul itself that wills nothing else than genuinely to live from the ground and to establish reality transfigures the lived world in the light of meaning into a holy mirror in which the sign of primal being appears. Orientation installs all happening in formulas, rules, connections which are useful in its province but remain cut off from a freer existence and unfruitful; realization relates each event to nothing other than its own content and just thereby shapes it into a sign of the eternal. As in his deed so too in his knowledge, the man who stands in the love of the world is related to the primitive man, to

the myth-creating man: as in myth a significant event of
nature or mankind, say the life of a hero, is not registered
in a knowable connection but is preserved as something
precious and consecrated in itself, adorned with the pride
of all the spheres and elevated as a meaningful constellation in the heaven of inward existence; and as there in
its exalted solitude it becomes a symbol of all fate and a
mirror of the faintly sensed world-spirit, so he who stands
in the love of the world does not know a part of a conti-
nuity but an event which is fully complete and formed in
itself, as a symbol and seal which bears all meaning. This
is meaning: the mythical truth of the unconstrained
knower who relates to each event in its content alone
and thus shapes it to a sign of the eternal. He receives
that which befalls him as a message; he does what is
necessary for him as a task and proclamation.

And thus according to man's concepts he has no image
of the world; in fact, he has one that is as immediate as
Veronica's handkerchief: in his life. He does not know
the world and does not know whether one can know it;
but the unknowable is authenticated for him as one lived
in him and through him. For like the primitive man,
who has in magic his essential deed, in myth his essential knowledge, and celebrates them as both covenant
with and festival of the mystery in which he conquers
separateness and unites himself with the God, so he
who has direction and meaning celebrates an ever-new
mystery in his realizing: to live so as to realize God in all
things. For God wills to be realized, and reality is God's

reality, and there is no reality except through the man who realizes himself and all being.

This is the kingdom of God, Reinold: the kingdom of danger and of risk, of eternal beginning and of eternal becoming, of opened spirit and of deep realization, the kingdom of holy insecurity.

Security—thus you name the breath of your first life. But that was not the security of those who protect themselves and know their way about. That was the security of the sleepwalker. Children are sleepwalkers in the world. They pass through all abysses unharmed, for they do not see them. The direction that guides their steps is dreamlike, the meaning in which everything fulfills itself for them is dreamlike. Dreamlike they realize their life-experience. It is granted them to realize without risk because they are unaware of the inner duality and therefore all things also offer themselves to them undivided. Everything harmonizes with them like a roundelay, and the contradiction itself joins in the play. If God wants to appear to them, he must disguise himself as a traveling musician and put on a foolish face.

Then comes the hour of awakening. It can come late. There are men whose realizing power is so great that it outlasts childhood in its first form—the dreamlike simplicity. No matter: it happens that an abyss that one has countless times passed by suddenly looms at his feet. The abyss of contradiction and of opposition: the abyss of the thousand-named immanent duality of all things. It calls to him out of the deep, and then he knows that an abyss in himself answers, it too thousand-named: the abyss of his inner division. Thus he is afraid. And in his fear the choice is placed before him: to which will he give the power, orientation or realization. This is not a question of delivering himself wholly to one: neither can exist without the other; it is a question of mastery. Orientation promises him security. Realization has nothing to promise. It says: If you wish to become mine, you must descend into this abyss. What wonder is it if the choosing man hands himself over to the friendlier mistress and only now and then, in the rare hours of self-recollection, casts a melancholy glance at the other?

You have decided, Reinold, whom you do not want to follow. Thus you have also already decided whom you want to follow. You have known from of old what you must do, and you also know it now; for direction is with you as of old. But this is the time when your first, dream-like strength is at an end and your second, awakened strength wants to commence. There you stand irresolute and lost in thought as though you listened to a distant call. Still the fact that you have today spoken with me is your first new step. Now you again know your way.

Meaning appeared to you to be burst, Reinold. That is because it wanted to renew itself. In the dreaming heart a daring heart was enclosed that wants now to arise, wants to awaken from its larva life to a winged life. The duality of the world was enveloped for you in the light of meaning; it advanced toward you out of it; now you shall envelop it anew in resurrected light. Thus meaning is reborn for you, and nothing can injure it henceforth.

Dreamlike until now the peace of your becoming, and now it is disturbed by restlessness and wandering. You must win it anew, and as an awakened one. It had light feet and a flowerlike glance, and it knew nothing of danger. Now you are dragged out with it and visited by dangers. And from every path it will return with stronger longing and steadier eyes. But be comforted: its feet will not unlearn the dance and its glance the caress.

Danger, danger, danger: that is from now on your path. "God and the dreams," so goes a song, Reinold, the song of the happy early ones. But your motto will be: God and danger. For danger is the door of deep reality, and reality is the highest price of life and God's eternal birth.

And if the poets of the age should surround me and each ask me: "Have I not imagined the most beautiful life?" then I would answer: The most beautiful life that has been imagined is the life of the knight Don Quixote who created danger where he did not find it. But more beautiful still is the lived life of him who finds danger in all the places where it is to be found, and it is to be found in all places. All creation stands on the edge of being; all creation is risk. He who does not risk his soul can only ape the creator.

Live upright and attentive, opened and devoted in the peace of your becoming, Reinold, and love danger. You have no security in the world, but you have direction and meaning, and God, who wants to be realized, the risking God, is near you at all times.

And this is your *nearest* danger: descend into the abyss! Realize it! Know its nature, the thousand-named, nameless polarity of all being, between piece and piece of the world, between thing and thing, between image and being, between the world and you, in the very heart of yourself, at all places, with its swinging tensions and its streaming reciprocity. Know the sign of the primal being in it. And know that here is your task: to create unity out of your and all duality, to establish unity in the world; not unity of the mixture, such as the secure ones invent, but fulfilled unity out of tension and stream, such as will serve the polar earth—the realized countenance of God illuminated out of tension and stream. But know too that this is the endless task, and that here no "once-for-all" is of value. You must descend ever anew into the transforming abyss, risk your soul ever anew, ever anew vowed to the holy insecurity.

IV

On Polarity

Dialogue after the Theater

LEONHARD: Did the play move you so, Daniel? As you walk next to me, imprisoned in silence, it feels to me as if we did not come the same way: I certainly from the theater, but you from Eleusis.

DANIEL: I come from the theater, Leonhard, and what has moved me and set me into a silence is the theater itself. I saw it today for the first time.

LEONHARD: You jest.

DANIEL: Has it not happened to you that you were acquainted with a man for many years and had him in and next to you, familiar as a word that you always have at hand and believe you know—although it has never occurred to you to regard it—and on an evening when the lamp between you and him stands in a new corner, you see him for the first time, and you are seized by wonder; for in the lines and proportions of the familiar face you recognize an unfathomable, significant secret—a ground line and ground proportion of life.

LEONHARD: And today you have seen the theater thus?

DANIEL: When I came in, it had just become dark.
How often already had I entered the auditorium at this
moment, and it had only added to my enjoyment that
I did not need to see anyone before the performance
began, and came out of the lax light of the street directly
into this severe light, out of the wild dice game of the
street directly into this regulated checker game. This
time it was different. In the darkness the event took hold
of me. Eleusis, you say; indeed, it might have been thus
with the consecrated when the lights were extinguished.
And then the curtain went up.

LEONHARD: But it was just then that the play began,
the play that I, sitting not far from you, have seen and
heard.

DANIEL: The play? Yes, somehow also the play; or, if
you will, first there began, in fact, only the play. But it
made itself felt so that something took place before me
in a way that seemed to me unusual and astonishing. In
a space that was lifted out of the context of space and no
longer had any connection, neither with the above nor
with the below, neither with the right nor with the left,
neither with the behind nor with . . . but yes, a single,
specific connection with this before where I was. In a
time that was detached from the course of time and fulfilled itself without before and after, and in each moment

was so filled with impetus and significance that it seemed to me that before and after had been emptied in order to fill this bulging vessel, the moment.

LEONHARD: But all round was still, indicated by the contrivances of the real space, the imaginary space out of which the men of the drama came and into which they returned, and into the drama there drifted and stormed, whispered and beckoned the imaginary before, the earlier life of these men!

DANIEL: It was not so to me. Rather, when they appeared to me, they came from the edge of being, and when they went, they died away into the void, as a tone dies away. They announced to me nothing other than their presence. And they did this with the precision of a shadow.

LEONHARD: How am I to understand you?

DANIEL: Look at the ground, at the shadows of the trees as they stretch themselves over our path. Have you ever seen in the upper world of the trees a branch so outlined, so clear, so abstract as here? Is that not the branchness of the branch? Shadows—and first of all I saw what I saw today in the theater like a shadow play: like an overly clear and still somehow unclear play. The intellectual prologue passed me by; I knew and did not know what happened.

I was like the youth in that fictitious issue of the Sopater.
Do you recall it? He has dreamed that he is consecrated
to Eleusis and that he sees the holy rites. Awake he
tells a friend, a consecrated one, what he has seen and
asks him whether it corresponds to the actual mystery.
The friend nods. Has he now betrayed the holy rites to
an unconsecrated man? No; for the dreamer had been
consecrated by the goddesses themselves, Demeter and
Kore, and as a consecrated one he had experienced all.
And yet he did not know; for he had not understood the
voice of the hierophant, and so the ultimate meaning of
the symbol remained unclear to him.

But suddenly I understood the voice that spoke within
me. And this all at once, as though the stage of this day
before which I sat had been transformed into the Christian mystery stage where the throne of heaven stood over
the human room, under which gaped the great devil's
maw of hell and the axis goes from pole to pole through
the heart of the poor sinners.

Yes, what I saw was the spectacle of duality. But not
good and evil; all valuation was only external dress.
Rather the primal duality itself, being and counterbeing, opposed to each other and bound to each other as
pole with pole, polar opposed and polar bound—the
free polarity of the human spirit. There outside in the
world of the lax light that I had left when I entered into
this kingdom of the severe, there outside the two were

enveloped by mediacy and unrecognizable; but here they stood naked and large as gods, naked their gestures, naked their voices. A mediating chorus of figures surrounded them, but they stepped forth from the mediating circle only clearer, more inaccessible still. What they did only unfolded what they were; the streams that ran back and forth between them only expressed but did not weaken the polar strength of their being thus; and what truly stood in the center between them was not something mediating but the I of the spirit whose primal secret duality they revealed.

LEONHARD: The play affected you so strongly?

DANIEL: The play . . . yes, it was certainly the play.

LEONHARD: It was performed with unusual force.

DANIEL: Yes, the performance too. . . . But at that time I knew nothing of play and performance. What happened to me at that time in the detached imaging to which my senses fastened was of so elemental a nature that I sensed no intention, no production, no arrangement; rather the happening that bestowed itself on me thus was immediately certain. But the two, the polar protagonists, had made a daimon—indeed, who then might know the silent names of the daimons! Now then, the daimon of the theater had magnified them for me. The cothurnus of the myth was strapped to their feet;

out of their dialogue resounded the antiphony of *ananke*.*
There they stood, the tragic pair, like Creon and An-
tigone, and had neither right nor wrong, neither guilt
nor innocence, had nothing except their being, their
polarity, their destiny. And I felt world-great before them,
as though I were the I of the spirit whose primal secret
duality they revealed. But already I was no longer before
them, rather truly in their midst, and the streams that
ran from pole to pole ran through my heart.

Then the curtain fell, the lights blazed up, a festive,
well-meaning light, fit to mediate between that of the
street and that which had now disappeared. I sat in the
midst of the audience and found it difficult to know
where I was.

LEONHARD: I know . . . I nodded to you, and you
greeted me in return, but as if you did not know me.

DANIEL: Certainly I did not know you. I knew nothing
except just that audience, but that truly and wonderfully.

I had, in fact, experienced what was the first act of
my drama not as one of the spectators but as a secret
hierophant; now the crowd of which I was a part sur-
prised me and filled me with astonishment as though
I had associated with it for the first time. These men

* Greek concept of irrational, irreducible necessity. [Translator]

had separated themselves out and combined; they had installed themselves in the solitary space, in the solitary time of this stage and accepted its procedure as something allied to them; with different meanings, to be sure, the one stirred to action, the other aware of the performance, only a few conjoined in that dynamic wholeness[*] in which the action and performance are submerged in a mythical reality, as symbol and preparation, but open to all that is happening to the actor, answering the symmetry of his step with the symmetry of the soul's step and, whether with resigned, whether with superior feeling, mastering a task.

So that "manifold and innumerable throng" was really like Eleusis which had represented the marriage of heaven and earth and the birth of God's son; and if they did not "regard as a salvation" what was presented, if their attitude was almost as profane as the chatting of their intermissions, they were still, as long as the stage spoke, united and revealed participants.

Their profanity did not withstand me. I still carried in myself the measure of that completed polarity in which I had stood for a while, like the measure of a passion that supplements everything fragmentary and broken around it to wholeness, rather lets it appear in its wholeness. So my surroundings grew together for me into a community

* Literally "in that dynamic wholeness of being-with (Mitsein)." [Translator]

of which I was a member. And thus, no longer as focus and center but as a member, I experienced the second act of my drama.

I perceived, as the member of a settlement of madre-pores may perceive, with the organs of the community; but at the same time this whole had become for me so unitedly present as a single being is present to himself in his consciousness. So, therefore, I found it, I found *myself* over against that other being who moved on the stage and conversed with himself. For without its weak-ening its inner cleavage, indeed at the very time when it had become more lively and stood more in relief, that polar world of the agon had also won the shape of a being. It stood over against my We-I, as the storm the stillness, the mountain of waves the sandy plain, the contradiction the agreement. But in all its multiplicity it still appeared to us now as a being like us, determined by a law and held together in its contradiction as we in our agreement. And so we extended ourselves over against each other, divided by the severe light of the footlights—space and frame, time and scene, agree-ment and decision, audience and tragedy—being and counterbeing.

Yes, being and counterbeing! For both stood in a polar relationship like those two on the stage; only they were less distinct because, crossing and troubling them, one other oscillated with them that I knew without being aware of it: the polarity of "appearance" and of "reality."

Being and counterbeing: but they were not set in
opposition to each other as the two in the drama who
now appeared to be enclosed in a unity; they did not
carry out their polarity as those did. Each persevered in
its calling, the one in happening, the other in perceiving. And this perceiving seemed to me no less notable
than that happening. For it did not behave with that
well-meaning neutrality that the observer commonly
brings to the observed. Rather it bore its oppositeness
in itself, in some way expressed, confirmed it; and not
just one part of that which had been divided in two
but the whole reality over against it. Therefore it sided
with no party; it was, as it were, itself a party which met
those two as a unity. But what a strange party which
was nothing but perception! Or perhaps still more than
this? Yes, something else was there: confirmation. And
confirmation, indeed, not of the mediating chorus that
also lived through the happenings on the stage, but of
the contradiction, the destiny, the decision. There stood
the two in the fury of their nature; there the fate worked
itself out between them; and here sat the audience and
confirmed, strengthened, affirmed; perceiving the fate,
it willed what it experienced. This awareness was a
proclamation.

Where had I already seen something like this? I recalled;
it was a crude early Greek vase-picture that shows the
psychostasia. Two heroes in battle, and behind them
Hermes weighing the souls. Coarsely as it is painted,
one sees: he does not take sides but his will follows the

decisions of the scales; he wills what must happen, and his will is a fanfare.

How this image appeared before my eyes, however, the difference between that and Hermes, agitated me violently. Yes, when on the stage the murdering knife is raised, the heart of this dark being, the audience, palpitates in the knife's point; but it quivers at the same time in the flesh that receives the blow. It joins with the fate that guides the hand of Oedipus, and it lives in the blinded eyes. It swings along with that wave that drives Lear to his madness; it circles in the pain of the king, mad like him.

And now I also saw it more clearly than before: before the great play all of them, those stirred to action and those aware of the performance, had a single heart in common. From the one fell off the firmness of his resignation, from the other the seeming force of his superiority; they became one in the act of inclusion.

For thus one may perhaps name what happened here. A being stands over against his counterbeing; it expresses, accompanying the impact of his fate, his polar being; but at the same time it throws itself across into his opposite pole and suffers his life with him. How shall one name this remaining with oneself and setting out, this desire to attack, and joy in sacrifice, this bipolar living? I say inclusion and know that I say too little. But allow me the word; for when I utter it I have another polarity in mind,

and the loving man is present to me who has a living experience not only of his struggling desire but also of the
blossoming beloved and includes what is opposite him as
primally his own.

The falling curtain called me out of these thoughts.
Again the festive, well-meaning light played over me,
and many detached men who were not at all members of
a unified whole stood, walked, ran around me. I stood up,
I went with them, then you came toward me.

LEONHARD: And when I stretched out my hand to you,
you asked me: "Do you not also wonder, Leonhard?"

"About what?" I said.

And you: "About the theater . . ." and with that you
smiled.

Then we spoke of other things, but I noticed that only
your friendly feeling was with me and talked to me.

DANIEL: Yes . . . for in the moment of my getting up
it struck me, by chance but with seriousness, that I had
to laugh at myself over what I had known all along and
yet had not known: that most self-evident, that most
inclusive, most trivial reality which this theater was.
That in the same moment as I and about me also these
men on the stage, the actors, many detached men, not
at all members of a unified whole, stood up, walked, ran,

relaxed and made preparations; that today they had come out of their houses in the twilight in order to act, as we out of ours in order to watch; that that whole that had just now been, was the fictitious life of an evening, and this piece that had now taken place was the real life of the generations.

But when that had become present to me thus, it was suddenly no longer trivial, but very singular and thought-provoking. Like one who for many years had had a house and was glad of it without reflecting on it and all of a sudden it strikes him: "That is a house," and he smiles. But only now does it begin to dawn on him what that is: a house; or like one who for many years lived with a wife and shared a common life with her, and all of a sudden it strikes him: "That is a wife," and he smiles. But only now does it begin to dawn on him what that is: a wife. Thus I felt. For what sort of a reality was this here which so loose and playlike surrounded me? And what sort of an appearance was that there that so severely and totally admonished me? Which was the deeper reality: the act or the inter-mission? And what sort of a power was that which drew the men out of the broken, mediated, blunted polarity of their lives and placed them before the pure, strong, direct polarity of the tragedy? And who were they who "acted" this essential reality? What did they do when they acted it? These questions oppressed me when I spoke with you and I could not free myself from them. Indeed, I could not wish to do so. Thus, full of questions I returned to my place, and the third act of my drama commenced.

Over the boards strode, I know not why and whither, a maiden on slender brown feet. Then something strange happened to me. Whatever else the stage was vanished, and I saw what I had often thought of but had never seen: the maiden that in Indian villages represents the harvest goddess Gauri, Siva's consort. A bunch of wild mimosa was carried before her, she walked on slender brown feet through all the rooms of the houses, and at the threshold of each room she was asked the question: "Gauri, Gauri, from where do you come and what do you see?" I know not what she answered. But in the last room the mistress of the house bows before her, offers her sweet sacrificial food and speaks: "Come with golden feet and stay forever."

LEONHARD: Is that not like the initiated saying to Mithras: "Remain with me in my soul"?

DANIEL: Yes, so it is. But Gauri is *represented*. How is that done? This maiden represents Gauri.

LEONHARD: Still not otherwise than a doll represents the one goddess. Whether the believer speaks to the statue of his God or the Indian wife to the living Gauri-doll, it is of the same nature; except that the divinity of the statue is probably believed in much more strongly than that of the maiden.

DANIEL: That may be; but the statue presumably has no consciousness. What made me thoughtful was the consciousness of the maiden. It represents the goddess. To be sure, it does not "act" it. But is it not in its inactive feeling still somehow moved? Is not its sleep blown by an incomprehensible breath of transformation?

LEONHARD: Perhaps. But it does not do anything other than what is assigned to it.

DANIEL: Are you so sure of that? That it does not hold the head a little more erect, hold the finger a little straighter, stretch the knee a little more tautly than otherwise? And is it ever assigned to a mortal being otherwise than as an ambiguous role that he must interpret with a single meaning in his action?

But my mind did not remain with Gauri. Once again before a curtain struck the stage, where a wedding had taken place, it wandered toward the north—or rather not so, instead it again emptied the stage and filled it with an ancient Nordic happening, and it too I saw only now. During the festive procession of Swedish peasants in which Freyr's statue is carried through the land along with that of the most beautiful virgin who is the bride of God, an unknown one breaks through and rides up to the holy carriage: similar to the God in shape, bearing, clothing, he receives the sacrificial offering of the people, marries the priestesses, blesses the land for fruitfulness.

Gunnar Helming, an outlaw from Norway. He—played the God.

LEONHARD: Yes, to deceive the faithful. This is the trick Jacob played on Esau.

DANIEL: Do you think that Jacob and Gunnar deceived with slippery souls like shopkeepers? That under the animal hide and the God's clothing the shudder of transformation did not overrun the body clothed with deceit?

But again, called up by the wedding dance, a new play stood before me: I saw the Bacchi on the stage. Not the Euripidean poetic production: the old Dionysus play itself which represented the *thiasos** and the nuptials, the passion and the resurrection of the God, and the souls so shook in eternal movement that today a grotesque rudiment still lives on in Thracian villages. I saw, in front of the horse-eared Satyrs and the snake-adorned Bacchic revelers, visible like a melodic column before the crudely shaped pillars, the young man who had been selected and had prepared himself to sacrifice his body for the body of the savior. Light and detached he stood before the dark intoxication of his companions; his foot struck the earth like the foot of a young steer; the streams of pallor and of blood mixed themselves on his skin like fire

* Procession of persons dancing and singing in honor of Bacchus. [Translator]

and water, and when his cheeks became red, they had
the color of new wine. In his eyes, however—which were
not seeing, only existing eyes—dwelt the transformations
"to winds and waters and stars and the birth of plants
and animals," and his free limbs completed it: freed from
all conditioning, they moved gently, stood shining, in
space, took root and strove. I recognized with holy heart
the hero of the souls. And he, the youth, more ingenious
than Gunnar Helming and more believing than the
Gauri-maiden—what was it that happened to him? What
was it that happened in him? Did not the secret of magic
rest on him to which all virginal peoples are devoted: he
who transforms himself into the God lives the life, does
the deed, works the work of the God? Did he not *realize*
the God in and with his soul as in and with his body?

When that had become clear to me, the face disappeared, and I again saw undivided the proceeding of the
theater. But less still than before did my glance want
to follow this breadth. It clung to one of the two protagonists who now stood to one side, leaning against a
solitary column, and regarded the tumult of the wedding
with folded arms. He was a man of high stature with a
wide chin and fine fingers. I gazed at him long and steadfastly; something veiled his being from me; thus clouds
lie around a cliff, and a weak sun can only disperse them,
not dissolve them. And suddenly I saw, now fully clear
and unveiled, *two* beings. Neither of the two resembled the man whom I had just now contemplated; both
resembled him. They stood in a twofold light; the one in

an unearthly, flashing white, like glacier snow at midday,
the other in a bluish, weak light, like autumn hills in the
evening mist. The flashing one had a forehead of cop-
per and eyes of emerald; his mouth was firm as a stone
bridge; his knee arched like the knee of kings. The weak
one had a forehead of brass and eyes of opal; his mouth
was stretched like a tightrope; his knee stretched itself
like the knee of a swimmer. The two stood over against
each other: I saw pole and opposite pole, being and
counterbeing in new form, and so keenly was I aware of
them that the hero at this hour could not be nearer my
heart than the actor.

Imagine a man, Leonhard, who breaks off his deed: who
lives only the soul's part of it, who feels that nameless
spark, that kinesis through which the deed from being
the life-experience of an individual becomes a happening
given to all: is he not similar to the doer and yet before
all his counterpart? For this fragment of the deed that
he lives receives the autonomy of a whole; it produces in
his feeling the illusion of a wholeness because it satisfies
his feeling; at first it was to him in its incompleteness a
phantom and a terror, now it becomes for him the bread
of life: from the fragment of the deed it becomes the
simulacrum of the deed. The deed stands like a sign on
the crossroads of the world; the simulacrum comes and
vanishes on the plains of the soul. The deed emerges out
of the darkness and is present, the simulacrum is fore-
known and measured. There are, however, men in whom
the existence which has not been worked out longs so

strongly for fulfillment that no illusion lasts for them. They shatter on their contradiction, or the simulacrum becomes creative in them; they complete it—training and making manifest the gifts of their body, their voice, their system of movement—through images, representations, doubles of the deed. They act the kinesis; they free themselves in their acting. But they can only do this when they transform themselves: for Lyaeus* their God blesses them, he who can only bless for hours and ever again only for hours.

LEONHARD: But are there not also other kinds and other ways?

DANIEL: No matter what kind and no matter what way, the great, the genuine actor always stands over against the hero as the simulacrum the deed, as the possible the actual, as the ambiguous the simple, as the roaming the striding: polar. And this situation would be poisoned and nefarious if he sought to weaken the opposition; if he crept after and aped the hero. But precisely this he does not do; rather in all consecration of polar distance he stands over against the hero and— transforms himself into him. That is the paradox of the great actor. Freed, purified, transfigured in the transformation, he realizes the hero in ever-new uniqueness with his soul as with his body.

* The releaser or deliverer from care, epithet of Bacchus. [Translator]

LEONHARD: You say "the great actor." So what you say does not hold true for all?

DANIEL: The little, the false actor, to whom the boldness of the simulacrum is alien, who stands over against the hero as the nothing stands opposite the something, fingers it with his senses; he collects the voice, the mien, the gestures of the hero; he traverses, explores, handles the world of the doer in order to acquire his material; and then constructs out of it a mask. But the great actor does not finger, he is transformed. Whether it is only the venturing genius of his simulacrum that helps him; whether it is demanded of him that he possess the hero in embryo in the all-possibility of his soul; whether, as I once dreamed it to myself, the daimon of an earlier life girdles and helmets him: the actor is transformed into the doer, the seeking into the acting, the wave into the way.

The great actor does not put on masks. In those formative hours in which he decisively lives his role, he penetrates—transforming himself, surrendering his soul and winning it back again—into the center of his hero and obtains from him the secret of the personal kinesis, the union of meaning and deed peculiar to him. Now he has the particular voice and gestures of the hero: because he has the element that commands and engenders them. He will become angry and bend forward, loose his scream; and noise and gesture are only in the timbre, their substance belongs to the man he plays, and only to him. Is he angry? He sounds the meaning of anger in himself, and the deed of anger resounds: because he has incarnated in himself their union, the personal kinesis.

LEONHARD: So the actor does not really experience the agitations that he acts?

DANIEL: He does not experience their feeling, but he experiences his action. And the excitement in which he stands is *his*: the excitement of the polarity, of the transformation. All high excitement has its origin in a polarity that is experienced, realized, carried out. Polarity is a task that can be carried out in many manners and on many ways. On whatever one this takes place— on the way of decision, on the way of inclusion, on the way of transformation—that high excitement which is above desire and pain, which is dearer and more sacred to the soul than desire and pain, bestows itself on the venturing man.

On whatever way it takes place. It may take place on the way of decision; that is the battle that is decided by genuinely faithful men on account of their desire for unity; decided acting—speaking—or keeping silent: so Francis of Assisi kept silent when the Spanish Dominic said to him, "Brother, I would that your rule and mine were one," and rejected the lower unity for the sake of the higher. Or it may take place on the way of inclusion; that is the love in which a genuinely present man embraces the creatures, so that he may live, remaining with himself in perfect power, the whistle of the tramp on his lips and the look of the fool in his eyes and, before he takes the poison drink, lament like Socrates the beautiful hair that the young Phaedo will sacrifice in mourning for him. Or it may take place on the way of transformation, that is, knowledge. For as the youth in the Bacchus play transforms himself into the God and realizes him, so the knower transforms himself into the world and realizes it. He cannot perceive its mystery with the senses nor inquire of it with thought; he can only penetrate it through transformation. Transformed, he executes with the movements of his existence the secret movement of the world: he lives the life of the world, he does its deed, he works its work—and so he knows it. For the secret of the world is the kinesis of the infinite, the union of meaning and being, and no one comes near it who reflects upon it: only he comes near it who does it; and he is the knower. He carries out the polarity in which he stands through realizing its opposite pole: through "finding" the meaning, as the Bacchic youth Dionysus and the actor the hero; the simulacrum that becomes creative in him is the imitation of the unknown God—which is realization. Thus through knowledge, as through conflict and through love, because a duality is fulfilled, unity is established out of it.

When I had become aware of this, I noticed that I no longer looked at the stage. I raised my eyes: there stood a man of high stature and looked, light and detached, after the departing wedding train. Nothing any longer

veiled from me his being; he was the son of venture and
of polarity; and he was beautiful.

Over this picture fell the curtain for the third time. I
leaned back, I was serene and thankful. And while I sat
leaning back the wings of this undirected thankfulness
bore me slowly through the world of the theater. But
since it found no one here who could wholly bear it,
it finally had to leave the theater and lift its flight into
the hiddenness. On the border of dreams, where heaven
and earth touch, it discovered the lonely wanderer
for whom it was valid without his knowing it. All this
time I had not thought of him, and yet it was his word
that the actors spoke, his bidding that their gestures
followed; Plato rightfully called them the messengers of
the poets.

His word—his bidding—and yet: was it really his work
that had been produced before me here, or had it not
rather been transposed into another species, another law,
another order? But on the other hand it seemed to me
just therein a fulfillment of his primal deep intentions;
as in every art, indeed, there dwell tendencies whose
ripeness no longer finds room in this art and must seek or
awaken another.

All poetry tends toward drama. Every lyric work is a
dialogue the partner of which speaks in a superhuman
language: what he says is the poet's secret. Every epic
work is a dialogue in which the Fates speak along with

the poet; to interpret for us their replies is the poet's task. The drama is pure dialogue; all feeling and all happening has in it become dialogue. It stands on the border of its art and points to that fulfillment and suspension in every other art in which the dialogue—is spoken.

It is he, the poet, who has made the actor speak. The strength of the poet is the word, the strength of the actor is the gesture; even speech is for him only a kind of gesture, and a later one. For among virginal peoples those who represent the divine wedding or the divine resurrection do not speak: they only dance; the aborigines on Swan River in Australia express the deepest truth of their souls when, to the surprise of the missionaries, they call the sacrament of the Last Supper a dance. And even at Eleusis only the hierophant spoke: until the poet came and released the voice of the actor for all time.

So I saw him, the master of the word, who moved the theater, and yet himself never really entered it. When the well-meaning light was extinguished and I knew: now the curtain will rise, I stood up and went softly out.

LEONHARD: What, you did not see the last act of the play?

DANIEL: I saw the last act of my drama. But how could I have remained? I had progressed with my thoughts to the border of dreams, to the poet; now I would be turned to and drawn away from the stage at the same time: to hear behind each word of each actor, even the most masterful, the gestureless, unaccented, untouched, the concise and secret, the essential-voiced word of the poem whose determined simplicity the splendid theater can only draw out, the faithful theater can only interpret; and behind the word of this poem the infinite word of the eternal poet would rustle for me, but not this or that and not all, rather the word of *the* poet: which I in this hour could only seek and will, but not behind the forms, rather in solitary spirit.

So I went out into the garden into whose mild darkness the moon-bow sent the arrow of a tender clearness. This pure light made me happy, this light that was neither lax nor severe but pure as the glance of a bird. Here I could think of the poet.

Of Enoch, who walked with Elohim, it is told that he had become one of the angels who was all eyes and wings. Thus is the poet. Everything in him perceives the things, and everything in him flies past the things. He is wholly in the one thing that he experiences, and yet is already and still in all the others at the same time. He knows the fervor of persevering like the painter and the fervor of soaring in air like the musician. His senses are the strongest anchor of the world, and his soul the most changeable keel. He drinks eternally, like the poet in the *Purgatorio*, out of both springs: Lethe and Mnemosyné, which Dante called Eunoe.

This duality in becoming of the poem appeared in new accent and effect. All action of man is, in fact, a mixture of creation and destruction, and every doer must, knowingly or unknowingly, reject the many that might arise through him for the sake of the one thing that he chooses; but this holds true of no one in so full a measure as the poet: because he incessantly decides. To write poetry is a choosing in the infinite; and this choosing is not a hunting, a seeking, a sifting, rather, it is a fire that has extinguishing and dissolving force. Each word of the poet is single; and yet there lies around each a ring of ungraspable material which represents the sphere of infinite vanishing; that is the track of the dissolving force of fire.

He whom Plato calls the messenger of the superpolar God is no less than this, the messenger of the polar earth. As in his deed the twofold stream that circulates in all living things manifests itself condensed and spiritualized, so there moves in his being, winged and aflame, all the tensions in which the soul of man erects itself, and every opposition, which otherwise is only sketched or blunted or accessible to mediation, is intensified in him to polarity. He knows the pole of exuberant strength and that of weakness, that of freedom and that of dependence, that of concentration and that of abandon, that of guilt and that of purity, that of form and that of formlessness: he recognizes them all in the world because he knows them in himself. Of Indra, the divine poet, who found in his songs dawn, sun, and fire, it is said that he holds all, embraces all, as the rim of the wheel embraces the spokes. Of the poet it can be said that his heart is the hub into which the spokes of polarities converge: here is not a suspension, however, but union, not indifference but fruitfulness. The poet bears the antitheses of the spirit, and in him they are fruitful. For he has a two-fold great love: the love of the world in which everything that he experiences in himself as extreme and contradiction blooms toward him in the innermost truth of colors and tones as in a wonderful reconciliation, and the love of the word which, born out of the deep tension of earlier human dreams, shaped into the deep tension of seeking human generations, can redeem and bring into harmony all tension. World and word: in the love of the poet they come together, in the love of the poet their love ascends, in their love all antitheses become fruitful. Fullness and emptiness engender in the poet, pain and joy engender in the poet, heaven and earth engender in the poet, word and world engender in the poet. *To speak the world*: that builds the rainbow bridge from pole to pole.

All poetry is dialogue: because all poetry is the shaping of a polarity. The unmediated polarity of the soul, that is the lyric situation: out of one of his pairs of opposites the poet has lifted the one pole to the absolute and addresses it, treating himself as the other pole. Or the mediated polarity of the world; that is the epic situation: the poet subordinates his love for the world, and the world ascends while the loving spirit stands over against it as that reconciliation in which even the Fates do not terrify. Or the dramatic: then the poet flings his burning contradiction into the world, and it stands in flames.

The polarity which man experiences in himself wills unity. And unity is not now or ever something which "is there"; unity is that which eternally becomes. Not out of the world: out of our action comes unity. The poet finds it where word and world engender in him: in his work; there he grounds all duality in unity. But out of each work polarity arises for him anew: renewed. Rejuvenated, sharpened, deepened, it summons him to new deed.

Thus the poet is the messenger of God and of the earth and is at home in the two spheres. The force of fire is his force; it burns in contradiction, and it shines in unity. Like Enoch, of whom a legend tells that he was transformed from flesh to fire; his bones are glowing coals, but his eyelashes are the splendor of the firmament.

V

On Unity

Dialogue by the Sea

LUKAS: It was a year ago today, Daniel, and that is the place where he climbed into his bark.

DANIEL: Tell me how it happened.

LUKAS: I had spoken to him in the evening. Rather, he had spoken to me. He stood by the sea, which was autumnal green and white as today, and looked with a still more tender gaze than usual at the water. Then he said: "Now the mother is free and no longer the maid of sun and heaven and may bear freely her own colors." You must know, Daniel, that he never called the sea anything else than the mother.

Early next morning he climbed at the usual hour into his bark. The beach was deserted, but Kajetan, who at that time lived in the tower over there, saw through the glass the bark with the yellow sail slowly swimming out as always. It struck him that Elias was not bent forward as usual, even when the wind was favorable, but sat leaning

back. He went below and asked the old Ubaldo what he
expected the wind to be like; then he returned into the
house and fussed a good while on a new violin that he
had almost ready. It was for its sake that he had arisen
so early. When he tried the tone he was dissatisfied,
although the tone was beautiful; then the bark occurred
to him again. He ran into the tower room, adjusted the
glass, and saw the bark far out. Elias knelt on the edge
of the bark, bent over, his arms extended perpendicular
to the water; his two hands stroked it ever again like the
limbs of a beloved being. Kajetan said to me that he had
to think of Empedocles at that moment: with such movement of the hands he had always imagined Empedocles.
That struck him so that he had to look away. When he
looked again, Elias was no longer in the bark. Kajetan
tore open the window, shouted something to the people
below, which they did not understand, and ran down the
stairs. It did not take long to send out a boat, but it took
very long until they found the corpse. They tried in vain
to awaken life in him.

DANIEL: It touched you closely as though a friend of
yours had died, and yet you hardly knew him.

LUKAS: Who could have known him? . . . But, Daniel,
never after the death of a friend have I experienced what
I experienced here.

Of grief I felt nothing, and nothing of a desire that he
might still spend life at my side. Rather his dying seemed

to me right and well done. Also I did not think about
the fact that he would be missing in my world; only that
he had as yet been missing somewhere and now filled his
place. The reality out of which he had once been broken in order that he might build himself a home in the
formative might of two human bodies had remained in-
complete until this moment when he returned, and now
he entered into it and supplemented it again to its existence. Supplemented? No: fulfilled it. For he entered into
it as a transformed one. Thirty years of earthly life—if
there are also spirits, then they remain unnoticed as the
fraction of a second is unnoticed by us—are a truth,
and when a man has completed them, then they are the
truth of truths. As a transformed one, as a completed
one, one ripened to a transforming strength he returned,
summoned to transform the mother herself. The old mystery shuddered through me out of the present. Was life a
ripening and death the entrance into a sphere of divine
deed before which earthly life only exists as a simile? But
for whom could this hold true except only the completed
man? Of those mythical creatures which are called cells
it is said that most of those in our bodies perish and only
a few become generative cells that have the capacity of
living on. May we grasp this explanation of the living as
a symbol of the superliving: are there also among men
those who perish and those who ripen to eternity?

But as I thought this, it seemed to me suddenly as
though I stood in Elias' bark and let down a sounding
lead into the water, and my thoughts appeared to me

an idle presumption, a *hybris* of unholy fantasy. Indeed, it was unholy to take away beforehand and forge an armor when he only fulfilled the direction of his highest hour, and dying genuinely carried through his life, when he entered the bottomless There naked and unarmed, without belief and without imagination, preserving only his readiness. I said to myself, There, and out of my own words the contradiction convulsively started up. How could there be a There if it was not also here? How could I become death's if I had not already now suffered it? My existence was no rolling ball that I could think of as stopping somewhere or preferably being thrown further. It was the bed in which two streams, coming from opposite directions, flowed to and in and over each other. There was not only in me a force that moved from the point of birth to the point of death or beyond; there was also a counterforce from death to birth, and each moment that I experienced as a living man had grown out of the mixture of the two—they mixed with each other like man and wife and created my being, and I never stood in the stream, but all the time in stream and opposing stream at once. What I *knew* was the stream coursing downward alone, but what I *was* comprehended the stream coursing downward and the stream coursing upward in one. A force bore me toward dying, and its flight I called time; but in my face blew a strange wind, and I did not know what name to give its flight. The two, whose vague image as it is projected into the shy mirror of our senses is called by us coming-to-be and passing-away, these two did not alternate with each other like building up and breaking down; they lay side by side in endless embrace, and each of my moments was their bed. It was foolish to wish to limit death to any particular moments of ceasing to be or of transformation; it was an ever-present might and the mother of being. Life engendered being, death received and bore it; life scattered its fullness, death preserved what it wished to retain. And this certitude was not unholy; it was, indeed, no feeling of being secure in any certainty but the unarmed trust in the infinite.

And this certitude, Daniel, I hold like the image of him who bequeathed it to me. But since I have again been on this beach and every yellow sail propounds to me anew the question of the world, a new unrest has come over me. For I feel morning after morning as though I journeyed out in Elias' bark, and those that once were enthroned for me in the poles of heaven, primally distant from each other so that my glance could never take in both of them at the same time, they sit quite near to me and to each other as fellows; with forehead bent forward the demon of life sits at the rudder and with head thrown back the goddess of death sits in the prow. Once it appeared enough to me to know about their existence—now that they have become familiar to me they have grown monstrous and agitating to my very heart: because I journey with them. From day to day the question mounts higher in me, what sort of a sea is it on which we travel, they and I, what sort of a sea has given birth to us, them and me. I know that in some way I am myself this sea, but I cannot reach there where I am it. And yet Elias reached there. Is what we call death, therefore, perhaps the way? To think that is senseless; what life did not accomplish, death too will not produce. Elias was *reached*; when he died, he expressed only the existing? But I? He is dead *for* me; how do I begin to live for him?

Once when they still appeared to me as boundaries, succeeding each other in service or play, these two satisfied me by their duality. Life handed me over to death as a letter that goes from runner to runner, life threw me to death like a torch that the hand touches only to fling it onward. It did not matter whether the receiver of the letter was near or far, it did not matter whether the torch moved into the infinite or was soon extinguished because of a sluggish player; it was simple and good to wander from life to death, and their doubleness was an ultimate and permanent state behind which I had no desire to look because it was the end and the consecration of my world. It has now become otherwise. Since these two are no longer boundaries but are in each other, since they are no longer over me but rule in me, an alternating movement no longer satisfies me; they drove me to penetrate behind them into the infinite that bears them both. As they work in me—through me—I listen, I am aware, I ask: what is the command? Now I know for certain that, destroying and shaping, they create my being, make out of what I actually am an essential being, and it did not occur to me to wish to know for what world of time or of eternity, of space or of spirit it is destined. But the unity that this creating commands and leads, that which bears life and death in right and left hand, that holy sea I want to know. I do not wish to grasp what is outside me, but I long to behold what I am.

DANIEL: Let me tell you an event out of my youth. I was seventeen years old when a man died whom I had loved. Death laid itself about my neck like a lasso. It seized me as the Christian God seizes a sinner who must atone in God's place. That there was dying in the world had become my sin for which I had to do penance. Because of my isolation I could take no sleep and because of my disgust with living I could tolerate no nourishment; I believed that this happened as a penance. My family, strengthened by friends and physicians, regarded me fussily and helplessly as a changeling. Only my father met me with a calm, collected glance that was so strong that he reached my heart, inaccessible to all other perceptions. It was also this man, silent but united with the future, who soon came to the special decision through which I was saved: he sent me all alone into a secluded mountain place. I believe that the great time that I lived through there will return once more in the images of my dying hour. The first day in the face of the mountains crumbled my foolishness and threw it to the winds. The blue glow of the arch of heaven, the towering pride of the earth and the contacts with that infinite free being that we call air and of which only a shadow is accorded to us in the plains, surrounded me like a working divine power. Now for the first time I recognized that I was separated; now for the first time I found myself before the eternal wall. And at the same time I knew that I could not come to my dead, not even through death, that he could not come to me, not even through birth; for I saw the deeds of the world on another level than that of the proclaimed truths. In the feeling that this knowledge was full, I now lived through the days, without consolation, but no longer losing myself as in the penance, rather winning myself through despair. For despair, Lukas, is the highest of God's messengers; it trains us into spirits that can create and decide.

One morning I had climbed a small Alp from which one looked down on an equally small lake enclosed by crags. This lake received my whole gaze and held it like a magic crystal. Soon the surrendered gaze was freighted with my forces and my movement. Relaxing I felt how everything in me went into it; it grew as I waned; and finally even the living power of grief, my orphaned state, went out of me—I was as little orphaned now as a newborn child whose mother has died. Thus I fell asleep. I still knew my glance to be hovering over the deep, then this too disappeared before the consuming nothingness. I slept in the timeless while the happening of the world meted out my hours.

The first thing that I sensed on awaking was a terrible, absurd, penetrating question about the lake. And yet—this was my next perception—yet I saw; but I saw nothing isolated any longer: I did not look. The power of selection of my glance had deserted me; I saw everything as a cloudy image in which all separateness dissolved. Light and dark were entangled in each other; all shape had stepped out of its boundaries and exploded into the iridescent snake-coil of the colors which had enclosed the spectral horizon. Fleeing from the unformed world, I relied upon my body and knew it as an island in the torrent of annihilations. Its firm being rested, bound and formed, in the midst of chaos, and yet in the most remarkable way was shattered and deformed by all things in its firmness. Instead of the streaming simplicity of the lived human image I found a twofoldness in myself: one half of me was life, the other had become death; in both I experienced not states but powers, here the command of the surging blood, there the compulsion of passing away. And while the movement of formation stormed through the one level, the spasm of disintegration jerked through the other. Both were so intensified to the uttermost, however, that my feeling lay below like an anvil and suffered the twofold hammer blows. And there, Lukas, at the uttermost, my soul arose in me. Not that seeming soul that thinks of self-preservation but the caretaker that wants completion. It trembled violently under the abomination of my cleavage and longed to go into the world in order to bring me unity. But in all the world it found only mixture and confusion, not unity. Then my body was inspired and did the simple deed: my two arms raised themselves, my hands bent to each other, my fingers entwined, and over all horror there

arched the God-powerful bridge. Then my body became
united, the world became one for me, my sight returned
to me unburdened: free and unencumbered I lay and
looked at the lake, which looked at me. And in this dou-
bly united gaze of giving and receiving I perceived that
I was no longer separated. I had torn down the eternal
wall, *the wall within me.* From life to death—from the living to the dead flowed the deep union. I could not come
to my dead, nor he to me, but we were united like the eye
and the lake: because I was united in myself.

In that hour, Lukas, the teaching came to me: the one
thing that is needful. It came to me mute and concealed,
like the grain of seed in the earth; it laid itself on my
breast and remained with me. I had it from that time
on, but I did not know it. On all wanderings I sensed
its presence, but I was not aware of it and had to march
from every journey into a new one. Until in a later hour
I marked that I had experienced it, without anything
happening other than that a moment joined itself to a
moment, even as what a little while ago was a bud in full
readiness is now a flower that has opened.

Since then I understood, Lukas: he who genuinely experiences the world experiences it as duality. He looks at it
neither with that close glance of the woman who cher-
ishes the little multiplicity of an enclosed foreground nor
with that distant glance of the man who subordinates
the things in the wave of a broad dynamic; he looks at
it with the glance of the human being: he grasps and

decides and brings forth out of the play of the manifold the essential line of tension. And to overcome this tension in his task.

The duality is many-named and multiform; differently known, it is different in circumference and significance; it remains the same in the tension. All wisdom of the ages has the duality of the world as its subject; its point of departure is to know it, its goal to overcome it. However it names the two forces that it makes known—spirit and matter, form and material, being and becoming, reason and will, positive and negative element, or with any of the other pair of names—it has in mind the overcoming of their tension, the unification of their duality. It seeks this through many ways, but none of its ways can satisfy him who is faithful to the totality of his life-experience. The longing for unity is the glowing ground of the soul, but he feels that he would degrade this longing if he surrendered something of the fullness of his life-experience to please it. He can only become obedient to it in truth if he serves it out of his completeness, strives to fulfill it out of his completeness, and thus preserves the experienced duality undiminished in the force of its distance. Therefore, none of the ways that the wisdom of the ages takes can satisfy him. That unity for the sake of which he must drown out the powerful voices of duality is not the right one for him; the tensions that he experienced in the storm he does not desire to do away with but to embrace. They have sketched his life with the diagram of greatness; only in them, out of them, with them can he penetrate to the greatest.

Each of the ways that the wisdom of the ages takes and that the seeker follows has become a wrong way for him; he must forsake each because he knows that to follow them he would have to forsake himself, the mystery of his life-experience. And so he wanders from way to way until in a later hour he comes upon the simple path of his self which is ready for him.

A wrong way, Lukas, was that sublime wisdom which commanded one to strip off the world of duality as the world of appearance, "like a snake skin," and to enter the world of unity, or rather to recognize himself as standing in it, as being it. For the faithful person wants unity not as one who turns away, not as torn from becoming, he wants it just as this human being who lives through the whole oscillation of duality, who receives and endures a terrible blessing. What does it matter to him henceforth that this is the world of illusion? He has measured its depths and may no longer deny his measure. Henceforth he will not retreat before the fluctuating, raging, whirling world of division and of contradiction; he will stand steadfast therein, in the midst of it stand steadfast and dare just out of it to derive and create unity. He will not go again into the wilderness where one needs only to annihilate in order to find; he does not want to annihilate but to fulfill, and he would rather renounce salvation

than to exclude Satan's kingdom from it. Not behind
the world but in the world will his unity be sought, for
what he seeks is not overcoming but completion, and he
who completes cannot desire to obliterate anything, to
weaken anything, to equalize anything.

And also a wrong way to the faithful man, Lukas, was
that upright wisdom that thought duality together into
unity. I mean those whose clear meaning it was to see
the two forces together, no matter in what form they
appear, as sides, as faces, as aspects and over the abyss
of duality to let the glory of identity shine forth. This
way, too, did not satisfy the faithful man. For if I perhaps
know that nature and idea are manifestations of one
single reality, is that reality then directly present to me
as unity, present in the midst of the elemental tension
of nature and idea that shatters my firm heart? Or if I
perhaps know that action and passion are expressions
of a single basic process, can it ever give and reveal
itself to me in the face of the hard gift and revelation of
those two which circle my fluctuating life like light and
darkness? I will honor them, these genuine thinkers, as I
honor those who have genuinely put aside becoming, but
I will not take their way. For their way leads aside from
the clattering highway on which I live and outside of
which I will not accept God.

Therefore, Lukas, the third way could also not benefit
the faithful one: that innermost wisdom that proclaims
that the awakened man indifferentiates all opposites and

all antinomies in himself. For like the suspension and
the equalization, neutrality also cannot be unity for him.
If the being of the world were perhaps designated as the
one end and the not-being or becoming of the world as
the other and the lived truth of the awakened man were
set in the middle, then this might well mean salvation
from suffering. But he who loses the ends and the swinging suffering has lost the flight and the song of his life,
the noble material of completed unity. If I were a bird,
says the faithful man, then I would not have life in my
belly but in my wings, and not in my balancing but in my
soaring. Or if I were a bell clapper, then I would want to
be aware of my soul when, ringing on my walls, I touched
one of them, not when I withstood them both. For his
place is not in compromise, but in decision, and as precious as the silence of heaven is to him, more precious to
him still is the organ playing of earth.

And yet, Lukas, each of the three wrong ways produced
truth in the faithful one, each ripened a layer of teaching
in him to conscious being. The first confirmed in him
the striving for unity, for what he beheld detached guar-
anteed him fulfillment: what yielded itself to him in the
formless depths that *was*, and because it was, it must also
arise for him out of the formed breadths; what revealed
itself to him in self-collectedness must prove itself true
for him in the scattered totality of his life-experience;
to that which he had unbecome out of the world, to just
that he must be able to become in the world—then only
was what he sought genuine.

And then came the second way and radiated unity for
him over the world, joined might to might and let them
cleave to each other like lovers, no, as the hollow of the
bow cleaves to its curve. Thus it was recognized, known,
and thought, but it was not reality for it was not lived.
But unity must be able to be lived, to be *realized*.

The third way undertook to realize it. All duality was
tested in its own being and unity sought with the whole
attitude of life in the world. But because the search took
place not in the extended swinging, but in the indifference, what was won was not unity fulfilled by all-being
but the independence of zero. The awakened man is
independent of all, not at one with all. The genuine,
completed unity can be nothing other than the man
all of whose tension is unified and in whom the world
unifies all its tension.

And now I shall tell you, Lukas, how the final level of
the teaching ripened in me and how the teaching arose.
But there is almost nothing more to tell. I said it to you
already, in fact: a moment joined itself to a moment. On
a gloomy morning I walked upon the highway, saw a
piece of mica lying, lifted it up and looked at it for a long
time; the day was no longer gloomy, so much light was
caught in the stone. And suddenly as I raised my eyes
from it, I realized that while I looked I had not been conscious of "object" and "subject"; in my looking the mica
and "I" had been one; in my looking I had tasted unity.
I looked at it again, the unity did not return. But there

it burned in me as though to create. I closed my eyes, I
gathered in my strength, I bound myself with my object,
I raised the mica into the kingdom of the existing. And
there, Lukas, I first felt: I, there I first was I.

The one who looked had not yet been I; only this man
here, this unified man, bore the name like a crown. Now
I perceived that first unity as the marble statue may
perceive the block out of which it was chiseled; it was the
undifferentiated, I was the unification. Still I did not understand myself; but then there flashed through me the
memory: thus had my body fifteen human years before
done the simple deed and, the fingers entwined, united
life and death to "I."

True unity cannot be found, it can only be created.
He who creates it realizes the unity of the world in the
unity of his soul. Thus beforehand he must live through
the tension of the world in his soul as his own soul's
tension.

Whenever the living soul experiences itself, it experiences itself as duality. Its unity is only a name, its multiplicity only an image; in all its movement, in all its
perceptions it experiences itself as duality, tension, task.
Knowing and feeling, acting and valuing, man stands
in the protean phenomenon of the inner polarity in
which the one pole is always directly present to him, the
other indirectly, the one is possessed by him, the other
is known about. Thus in him the tension is made ready

which he shall broaden to the all-tension. The inner polarity is the vessel that is filled with the smallest content and yet can contain the infinite: he who wills to create unity fills it with infinity.

He takes the tension of the world upon himself so that it is lived by his soul as its own. He takes upon himself, say, the tension of spirit and matter, and the soul experiences world-wide its own freedom and its own bondage, its own spontaneity and its own being conditioned, its own bearing and its own being borne. It is no longer so that the one pole is present, the other only known about, but in it there takes place simultaneously the full polarity in undiminished brilliance and strength. The man takes the tension of material and form upon himself, and the soul experiences world-wide its own wildness and its own taming, its own fullness and its own shape, its own chaos and its own cosmos. It comprehends in itself action and suffering at once, and the stream between the two that streams through it is the stream of the eternal powers. The man takes upon himself the tension of being and becoming, and the soul experiences world-wide its own stillness and its own movement, its own fixity and its own whirl, its own continuance and its own transformation. The two aspects of the great nature stand with each other in the outstretched heaven of the living soul. Thus the world lives its duality from within: in the man who wills to create the unity.

He creates it by bringing together in himself the tension that he has taken upon him: *by awakening the I of this tension.*

There is in reality no I except the I of a tension: in which it brings itself together. No pole, no force, no thing—only polarity, only stream, only unification can become I.

Look before you, Lukas: it is ebb tide. Can the ebb tide say I? Or the flood tide? But imagine the sea to have a spirit that comprehends in itself the unity of ebb and flood: it could say I.

The mica could not say it; he who looked at it could not say it; and the undifferentiated of its first look was only material. But when it had brought its tension together, the unified could say I.

What we commonly mean by "I" is a starting point and expedient, a grammatical fact. But the I of the tension is work and reality.

We live so much the more really, so much the more individually the greater tension we realize as "I." In this increasing measure the I comes into being in us.

To live the tension of the world is the highest test of our being.

Experiencing freedom and bondage in one as one's own, the soul brings forth the I that embraces freedom and bondage as its functions. Fulfilling timelessly the swinging of fullness and form, the soul summons the I that bears fullness and form as its limbs. Uniting continuance and transformation in the all-present, the soul awakens the I that possesses continuance and transformation as its gestures.

This I is the I of the world. In it unity is fulfilled. This I is the unconditioned. And this I is inextricably inserted in a human life. Human life cannot escape the conditioned. But the unconditioned stands ineffaceably inscribed in the heart of the world.

The sum of a life is the sum of its unconditionedness. The might of a life is the might of its unity. He who dies in the completed unity of his life utters the I that is not inserted, that is the naked eternity.

We spoke of death, my friend Lukas; we have all the time spoken of nothing else. You wish to know the holy sea, the unity that bears life and death in right and left hand. You cannot know it otherwise than when you take upon yourself the tension of life and death and live through the life and death of the world as your life and your death. Then the I of this tension will awaken in you—the unconditioned, the unity of life and death.